KEEP YOUR HAND ON THE PLOW

THE AFRICAN AMERICAN PRESENCE IN THE CATHOLIC CHURCH

United States Catholic Conference • Washington, D.C.

Keep Your

HAND

on the

PLOW

COMMITTEE ON AFRICAN AMERICAN CATHOLICS
NATIONAL CONFERENCE OF CATHOLIC BISHOPS

OFFICE OF RESEARCH
UNITED STATES CATHOLIC CONFERENCE

In its 1993 and 1994 planning documents, the Secretariat for African American Catholics, in collaboration with the USCC Office of Research, was authorized to address issues affecting African American Catholics. The present document, *Keep Your Hand on the Plow: The African American Presence in the Catholic Church*, was approved by the members of the Bishops' Committee on African American Catholics in March 1995 and is authorized for publication by the undersigned.

> Monsignor Dennis M. Schnurr
> General Secretary
> NCCB/USCC

Photo Credits: p. v, Michael Hoyt/*The Catholic Standard*; p. 20, Margaret Nelson/CNS; pp. 27, 101, Secretariat for African American Catholics; p. 61, Catholic News Service.

ISBN 1-55586-098-2
First printing, October 1996

CONTENTS

THIS BOOK IS DEDICATED TO

ARCHBISHOP JAMES LYKE, OFM,

WHOSE GENTLE SPIRIT

INSPIRED ITS WRITING.

Archbishop James Lyke

PREFACE

When the Lilly Endowment first came to the National Conference of Catholic Bishops (NCCB) and offered to fund a study of multiculturalism, it had in mind a study of Hispanics. It was deeply concerned, and rightfully so, about their growth and their future in the Catholic Church. The grant was to focus solely on this culture.

In a conversation about this with a bishop from a southern diocese, he was quick to point out that even though his diocese was experiencing a large increase in Hispanics, we should not overlook African Americans. He reminded us, "Keep a balance in your approach to multicultural expansion; don't focus so much on one culture as to overlook another!"

Thanks to this suggestion and the permission of the Lilly Endowment, the grant was re-directed toward producing a series of three books which would focus on Hispanics, African Americans, and Asians.

We are indebted to the NCCB Committee on African American Catholics for embracing this project with the USCC Office of Research, which is charged with advising the bishops of the United States on efforts of evangelization within the African American community.

We are particularly grateful to Rev. O. Hugh Stout for serving as editor of this publication. In addition, we are grateful to Therese Wilson Favors and Sr. Mary Alice Chineworth, OSP, who provided insights from the African American community and editorial assistance.

> Most Rev. Curtis J. Guillory, SVD
> Bishop of Galveston-Houston
> Chairman
> Bishops' Committee on African American Catholics
>
> Rev. Eugene Hemrick
> United States Catholic Conference
> Office of Research

INTRODUCTION

MOST REV. CURTIS J. GUILLORY, SVD

"And Jesus said . . . keep your hand to the plow." (Lk 9:62)

One of the most interesting and faith-filled stories within the Catholic Church in America is that which has been written by African American Catholics. They kept their hands on the plow of faith and their eyes fixed on Jesus. They were persistent and persevered under discouraging times. They were not distracted when faced with societal ills and moral misjudgments that forged rocky fields and thorny patches. They kept their hands on the plow when dark shadows of racism clouded the field. With great self-determination and steadfast activism, African Americans carved a place for themselves within the Catholic Church in America. They kept moving forward, planting seeds everywhere. They established religious orders, formed the first lay religious organization, and called forth vocations at the same time as they built churches and schools. They kept plunging forward, confronting the contradictions that existed within the institution. For only a people who know what they want to plant can look forward to a fruitful future. This document records the fruits of their labors. It reveals the direction of present-day issues that impact evangelization among African Americans. It is a poignant reminder that African American Catholics expect a future in this Church even though much of their history bespeaks of a time when the Church overlooked their mission, their efforts, and their unique gifts. It is a story that depicts the decisive unity of souls now gone who kept their hands on the plow. It is also the story of those today whose hands are on the plow, unearthing new grounds to be explored so that the Church may flourish and grow.

In "Catholic African Americans: A Historical Summary" noted historian Rev. Cyprian Davis, OSB, provides a historical prospectus of African American Catholic life. Fr. Davis documents the achievements, disappointments, and challenges experienced by African American Catholics today and in the future. His historical investigations reveal the "steadfast nature" of African Americans and provides a discussion of and direction for evangelization within the African American community.

As evangelization among African Americans is studied, a discussion on the African American family becomes a must. The family is the "domestic church"; thus this chapter is included. In "Understanding African American Family Realities," Dr. Andrew Billingsley discusses how faith communities and religious activity has supported the African American family. Dr. Billingsley encourages the establishment of church-centered outreach programs to strengthen and stabilize African American families. Some church programs are featured in this chapter.

The establishment and affirmation of indigenous leaders holds a strong place within the advancement or disruption of evangelization. Factors that prohibit as well as promote the development of such indigenous leaders are discussed. "A National Study of African American Priests and Seminarians" provides interesting data as the discussion of evangelization among African Americans is pursued.

This book also showcases several parishes that have conducted evangelization efforts among African Americans. The reader will see at least five characteristics they share: (1) a charismatic leader; (2) a strong social agenda that is scripturally motivated; (3) strong lay leadership from the congregation; (4) investment in youth and Catholic schools; and (5) creation and vigorous activation of Africentric programs.

The book concludes with a list of resources for African Americans, which contains information on

Catholic, non-Catholic, and secular resources, as well as a bibliography.

A document of this nature is important because it serves as a sharp reminder that African American culture should not be forgotten again amidst the multicultural expansion we are now experiencing. The intended audiences for this book are bishops, parishes, national forums, diocesan agencies, university students, researchers, and the like—all who are deeply interested or involved in multicultural expansion.

As evangelization among African Americans is studied and discussed, this document reminds us not to forget that racism, which has plagued African Americans, is still alive and at the root of poverty, poor education, sickness, and violence. In the 1984 document *For the Love of One Another*, Bishop Joseph A. Francis, SVD, in referring to the 1979 bishops pastoral *Brothers and Sisters to Us*, states, "It would be comforting to millions of people of all races if I could relate that the pastoral on racism has made a significant difference in the racial attitudes and practices of sisters and brothers in the Catholic Church in the United States. I fear it has not. In fact, I have often called it the 'best kept secret' in the U.S. Church."

The God of justice is glorified when people act justly. African Americans have called the Church to seriously examine racism and have reminded the Church of the suffering that injustices inflict. They have kept their hand on the plow. As we move into the third millennium it is hoped that Catholic universities and colleges expand, *as soon as possible*, their research on African American culture, and that all Catholic schools, parish adult education courses, and the like enlarge their curricula with African American studies. With this initiative, the entire Church will be enriched.

BLACK CATHOLICS IN AMERICA: A DOCUMENTATION OVERVIEW

DAVID GIBSON

INTRODUCTION

Sr. Thea Bowman, a Franciscan Sister of Perpetual Adoration, was enduring the advanced stages of bone cancer when she addressed the U.S. bishops in June 1989 at Seton Hall University in South Orange, N.J. The widely known teacher, author, and evangelist, who was director of intercultural awareness in the Diocese of Jackson, Miss., spoke from a wheelchair, but with great energy, to an audience that received and welcomed her enthusiastically.

"See, you-all talk about what you have to do if you want to be a multicultural Church: Sometimes I do things your way; sometimes you do things mine. Is that it?" Sr. Bowman asked rhetorically.

Many people have tried to sum up what a multicultural Church is all about, but that day Sr. Bowman did so uniquely as she described what it means to be both Black and Catholic.

"To the Americas our people brought the secret memory of Africa, the celebration of life values in an African way and style," Sr. Bowman told the bishops. "African ways of laughing and being together and loving: That's culture," she explained. However, as she traveled throughout the United States, Sr. Bowman said she saw Black people in the Church "who are invisible. . . . They are not consulted. They are not included."

What the Church's people need to do is "to walk together," she said. "If we as a Church walk together, don't let nobody separate you. . . . The Church teaches us that the Church is a family. It is a family of families, and the family got to stay together."

With those last comments, Sr. Bowman reached her presentation's conclusion. But then she did something unforgettable. She invited her audience of bishops to join her in singing "We Shall Overcome," asking them at the same time to join hands after crossing their right hand over their left. "You've got to move together to do that!" she exclaimed. Immediately she repeated those words:

> You've got to move together to do that! . . . See, in the old days you had to tighten up so that when

1

the bullets would come, so that when the tear gas would come, so that when the dogs would come, so that when the horses would come, so that when the tanks would come, brothers and sisters would not be separated from one another.

And you remember what they did with the clergy and the bishops in those old days, where they'd put them? Right up in front, to lead the people in solidarity with our brothers and sisters in the Church who suffer in South Africa, who suffer in Poland, who suffer in Ireland, who suffer in Nicaragua, in Guatemala, in Northern Ireland, all over this world. We shall live in love.

The singing resumed then, but now the words, "We shall live in love. . . . Deep in my heart, I know, I do believe, we shall live in love." When the verse concluded, Sr. Bowman's address concluded too, with these words: "That's all we've got to do: love the Lord, to love our neighbor. Amen. Amen. Amen. Amen."

I was asked as editor of *Origins*, the documentary weekly that Catholic News Service publishes, to contribute to this collection of materials by reviewing documentation *Origins* has published on Black Catholics in the United States. Repeatedly, that documentation calls for the full participation of Black Catholics in the life of the Church, a greater appreciation and inclusion of their gifts in liturgical celebrations and in the work of evangelization, and efforts to achieve a balance of unity and diversity in a multicultural Church.

MULTICULTURALISM: STRANGERS NO MORE

Sr. Bowman had a point to make: that the Church in the United States faces the risk that brothers and sisters may remain divided, may remain strangers to each other. She did her part that day in 1989 to draw people together.

This risk that people within the Church will remain strangers to each other is not confined to Catholics in the United States, of course. The universal Church today is contending with the

challenge this poses. It is a concern underlying conversations on the interrelated themes of "the multicultural Church," "inculturation of the faith" and "unity in the midst of diversity."

In her address, Sr. Bowman could speak almost in one breath of the invisibility of Black Catholics in the Church and of the need to foster a multicultural Church; of "being a second- or third-class citizen of the holy city," on the one hand, and of coming to the Church "fully functioning," on the other hand. When the processes of a multicultural Church are carried forward, the Church's people can begin to really see and hear each other and thus stop being strangers to each other.

But balancing unity and diversity in a multicultural Church, where "sometimes I do things your way; sometimes you do things mine," constitutes a difficult challenge, to judge by the considerable body of documentation devoted to the subject in recent years.

"The Church, in spite of eloquent statements, has not yet found successful ways of bringing peoples of various ethnic, racial, and linguistic groups into true fellowship and charity," Bishop Wilton Gregory, now the bishop of Belleville, Ill., said in a 1989 speech.

"How do people within a culture express diversity without being accused of being divisive?" Bishop Gregory asked.

His speech analyzed the challenge underlying developments that occurred during the summer of 1989 when a Black priest in the Archdiocese of Washington, George Stallings Jr., established Imani Temple, an African American Catholic congregation noted for liturgical celebrations reflecting the spirituality and customs of its congregation. Later Fr. Stallings was to announce that Imani Temple was separating from communion with the pope and the Roman Catholic Church, a statement confirmed when the Washington Archdiocese said that by his action "Fr. Stallings has excommunicated himself." In the summer of 1989, however, many voices were attempting to pinpoint precisely what challenge

Imani Temple was posing to the larger Church. Did Imani Temple point out the need for a new liturgical rite to serve Black Catholics? Was that the real issue, especially if, as some Black Catholic leaders observed at the time, other Black parishes could be singled out for effectively identifying with the customs and spirituality of their people, including parishes in Washington, D.C.?

"In a sense, the challenge to the Church is to embrace not simply a style of worship, but to endorse positively the culture from which such celebrations emanate," Bishop Gregory said. And he observed, "Tragically, we are still relative strangers to one another."

Brothers and sisters who are strangers to each other, who do not really know each other. That's how the Church's own members of differing races are described frequently enough.

What is to be done when brothers and sisters are strangers? Many propose that greater efforts to inculturate faith represent at least part of the answer.

For one thing, "it is essential that pastors and parish associates working within the African American community become familiar with the richness of African American art and music—as well as the art and music of other Black cultures," the U.S. bishops urged in a November 1989 statement titled *Here I Am, Send Me: A Conference Response to the Evangelization of African Americans and the National Black Catholic Pastoral Plan.*

The bishops said: "African American Catholics have become a recognized and articulate component of the Church in the United States. There is a vitality and an enthusiasm in the African American Catholic community." Elements of the culture of people who are Black "should not be foreign to the worship and ministry of the local parish and the local church," said the bishops.

Archbishop James Lyke of Atlanta, who died of cancer December 27, 1992, at the age of 53, once indicated (he was auxiliary bishop of Cleveland at the time) that to support legitimate inculturation of the faith among Black Catholics and to overcome a situation in which members of the Church are strangers to one another, it is necessary to appoint "pastors who want to minister in the African American community, are truly open to our culture in its various expressions, are willing to study formally the history and culture of our people . . . and enter the Black community as listeners and learners in order to be good pastors and teachers in the faith."

Archbishop Lyke was among the Black Catholic leaders who in 1989 were assessing developments surrounding Imani Temple. Speaking to Cleveland's Diocesan Black Catholic Advisory Board, then-Bishop Lyke said:

> There is no doubt that, if the Church in the United States is to adequately reflect the future complexion of its population, it will need to have more bishops of various ethnic backgrounds, particularly of African American, Hispanic, and Asian backgrounds. This principle of the indigenization of the clerical leadership is an ancient one in the missionary activity of the Church and is no less true today.

Bishop Lyke acknowledged in that address that "there has been much progress in the area of inculturation—in liturgy, sacramental preparation, catechesis, art, elementary school disciplines, and other facets of Church life." Nonetheless, he added, "once in a while I am shocked back to reality."

What is the underlying issue here? For Sr. Bowman, the issue was what it means to be both Black and Catholic. It means "that I come to my Church fully functioning," she insisted, quickly following up with a question: "That doesn't frighten you, does it?" She said that to come to the Church as a fully functioning person means "I bring myself, my Black self, all that I am, all that I have, all that I hope to become. I bring my whole history, my traditions, my experience, my culture, my African American song and dance and gesture and movement and teaching and preaching and healing and responsibility as gift to the Church."

What's more, Sr. Bowman said, "I bring a spirituality that . . . is contemplative and biblical and holistic, bringing to religion a totality of minds and imagination, of memory, of feeling and passion and emotion and intensity, of faith that is embodied, incarnate praise, a spirituality that knows how to find joy even in the time of sorrow, that steps out in faith, that leans on the Lord; a spirituality that is communal, that tries to walk and talk and work and pray and play together—even with the bishops."

Yes, even with the bishops. Sr. Bowman affirmed to her audience of bishops that fully functioning Black Catholics love all bishops. But she added, speaking of Black bishops specifically, "They are ours, we raised them, they came from our community and in a unique way they can speak for us and to us." She added: "Indigenous leadership. The leaders are supposed to look like their folks. Ain't that what the Church says?"

COMPLETING AN EQUATION

Addressing the special Synod of Bishops for Africa in Rome, Bishop J. Terry Steib of Memphis, Tenn., a Black Catholic bishop in the United States and a papal appointee to the synod, took notice of "a renewed attention by African Americans to their African heritage."

Bishop Steib said that "as a result of the civil rights movement, Black Catholics began to rediscover their African roots as a community within the Catholic Church. . . . Today, the African American Catholic community, taking strength and inspiration from its African roots, has a profound solidarity with the Catholic Church in Africa."

Evangelization, the synod's theme, led Bishop Steib to recall that "in 1984 the African American bishops announced a new era for African American Catholics." He said, "We, too, are convinced that it is time to be evangelizers ourselves." Bishop Steib was referring to *What We Have Seen and Heard*, a 1984 pastoral letter on evangelization issued by the ten Black U.S. bishops in September 1984. Part I of that pastoral was subtitled "The Gifts We Share." It began:

There is a richness in our Black experience that we must share with the entire people of God. These are gifts that are part of an African past. For we have heard with Black ears and we have seen with Black eyes and we have understood with an African heart. We thank God for the gifts of our Catholic faith, and we give thanks for the gifts of our Blackness. In all humility we turn to the whole Church that it might share our gifts.

Why emphasize these remarks here? Because documentation in the pages of *Origins* points again and again to the gifts found among Black Catholics, to their active role as evangelizers and to the contribution they can make to the Church at large.

One interesting discussion of this giftedness is found in Archbishop James Lyke's message to the 1992 National Black Catholic Congress. "The Catholic Church can learn a great deal from the larger notion of family that many people of color cherish," he said.

Archbishop Lyke was not able to attend the congress in person since he was undergoing cancer treatment at the time. But his message on the family—the congress's theme—was forceful. He discussed some of the most painful family situations born of injustice, poverty, racism. But he cautioned his hearers: "Please do not misunderstand me. We do not see only this. By no means! But it is this that cries out for the compassion of Christ." Then he said, "In African American communities there is a great capacity for compassion and accepting love. . . . Children born in situations that are far from ideal can be welcomed, cared for, nurtured, and loved. In my pastoral on family life, I noted this significant gift of Black family culture." Naturally, many pastoral letters and speeches in *Origins* attempt to raise awareness among Catholics of the effects of oppression and to promote justice toward Black people. At the same time, those goals are balanced in the documentation by a focus on the many gifts that Blacks—in all their own diversity—offer.

In this relatively brief essay I cannot cover every important point about Black Catholics discussed in

Origins' 23-year existence. However, I do want to review the repeated appearance in the documentation of these twin priorities: promoting justice "toward" and receiving gifts "from" Black Catholics.

What I conclude is this: There is much to suggest that the work of pastoral planners, catechists and other teachers, social justice ministers and, yes, writers and journalists, is incomplete if one part of this equation is left out—if, say, a discussion of ways "to serve" human needs omits the need of the larger Church to be enriched by Black Catholics— "to be served by" them. One might say that the documentation views ministry as a two-way street where everyone is the beneficiary of the gifts of others.

Before moving on, I want to recall quickly what the Black bishops said in *What We Have Seen and Heard* about "Black initiative," for the leadership Black Catholics offer in the work of evangelization represents an important concern of recent documentation.

The bishops insisted that the Black community is in a "privileged position to gain access to the hearts and minds of the African American community." Thus, they said, "we have the solemn responsibility to take the lead in the Church's work within the Black community." Black Catholics bear a responsibility both "to our own people and to our own Church," the bishops commented. "To the former, we owe the witness of our faith in Christ and in his body, the Church. To the latter, we owe this witness of faith as well as the unstinting labor to denounce racism as a sin and to work for justice and inner renewal."

Which leads me to a discussion of racism, certainly a major theme of documentation in *Origins* on Black Catholics in America. Returning for a moment to Archbishop Lyke's message to the 1992 National Black Catholic Congress, I recall him saying: "It is not enough for us as bishops to address our concerns about Black families to the secular and civil society. If we are to be credible we must speak first and loudest to our own Church where the sin and heresy of racism still endure."

RACISM

The memory of an estimated 11 million Africans once sold into slavery in North and South America—"victims of a shameful commerce"— was honored by Pope John Paul II when he visited the Slave House on the Senegalese island of Goree on February 22, 1992. "Throughout a whole period of the history of the African continent, Black men, women, and children were led to this narrow strip, torn from their land, separated from their relatives, to be sold as merchandise," the pope said.

"How can one forget the enormous suffering inflicted—ignoring the most basic human rights—on the populations deported from the African continent? How can one forget the human lives destroyed by slavery?" he asked.

This slave trade was a "human sin against human beings," a "human sin against God," Pope John Paul added. Taking note that baptized people participated in this sin, his visit to Goree became an opportunity to "implore heaven's forgiveness" and to "pray that in the future Christ's disciples may show themselves absolutely faithful to the observance of the commandment of brotherly love left them by their master."

By insisting that the African slave trade was sinful, and by challenging the human family's members to "learn to look at themselves and to respect themselves as images of God and to finally love each other as sons and daughters of the same heavenly Father," the pope's remarks in Goree embodied key themes in the Church's continuing discussion of racism.

When church leaders discuss racism, their goal is frequently to increase awareness among Catholics that
- Racism still exists.
- Racism is sinful.
- Racism represents a failure to recognize the human dignity of people created in God's image and redeemed by Jesus Christ.

RACISM'S CONTINUED EXISTENCE

"Today racism has not disappeared. There are even troubling new manifestations of it here and there in various forms," the Pontifical Council for Justice and Peace said in 1989. In a document titled *The Church and Racism: Toward a More Fraternal Society,* the council examined the reality of racism on a worldwide scale.

According to the pontifical council, racism's victims "are certain groups of persons whose physical appearance or ethnic, cultural, or religious characteristics are different from those of the dominant group and are interpreted by the latter as being signs of an innate and definitive inferiority, thereby justifying all discriminatory practices in their regard."

Actually, racial discrimination and racism continue to exist as "potent—and lethal—realities," Cardinal Roger Mahony of Los Angeles noted after the days of crisis in that city following the April 29, 1992, verdict acquitting police officers in the videotaped beating of Rodney King. Cardinal Mahony added: "With our vast ethnic diversity, we had hoped that we were learning how to live with one another as equals under God's providence. We were obviously mistaken in this assumption."

About the same time, Jerome Ernst, then executive director of the National Catholic Conference for Interracial Justice, had this to say:

> Much progress has been made on race in the United States due to the tremendous efforts of the 1960s, but in many ways this progress has been superficial and has not dealt with underlying causes. Many people have felt that the question of race had actually been resolved, but the dramatically shifting changes in our economy beginning in the 1970s and the crass materialism and selfishness of the 1980s have brought us back in so many ways to the environment of the pre-civil rights era.

Racism continues not only within society at large, but within the Church too, church leaders say. In November 1985, the nation's Black Catholic bishops presented a statement to the U.S. bishops' meeting in Washington saying:

There is evidence that just as some White Americans continue to feel that to have Black neighbors, Black co-workers, and Black classmates will be disruptive of their value system and their familiar patterns of life, some White Catholics feel that it will be equally disruptive to share the Scriptures, the bread of life and the cup of salvation with Black Catholics. As a result, when White Catholics pass through Black neighborhoods, they may feel sorry for Black people, feel afraid of them, or even feel guilty about their plight. But they do not welcome the call of the Spirit to invite their Black sisters and brothers to the table of the Lord. Consequently, many Black Americans still feel unwelcome in the Catholic Church.

The Black bishops added that "Black Catholics are very aware of how much the Church has done and continues to do on behalf of Black people." However, they said, "at this time when so many Black Americans are not associated with any church or religion, we believe that a special outreach and expression of welcome could have a tremendous impact."

In their 1979 pastoral on racism, *Brothers and Sisters to Us,* the U.S. bishops described racism as "an evil which endures in our society and in our Church. Despite apparent advances and even significant changes in the last two decades, the reality of racism remains. In large part it is only the external appearances which have changed."

About five years later, Auxiliary Bishop Joseph Francis of Newark, N.J., addressed the U.S. bishops and called *Brothers and Sisters to Us* the Church's "best-kept secret."

Bishop Francis, one of the nation's Black Catholic leaders, said: "The important message of the pastoral on racism is that racism is a sin and racism is a reality in our country and within our Church."

RACISM'S SINFULNESS

Brothers and Sisters to Us forcefully communicated the message that racism is sinful. "Racism is a sin: a sin that divides the human family, blots out the image of God among specific members of that family and violates the fundamental human dignity of those called to be children of the same Father. It described racism as "the sin that says some human beings are inherently superior and others essentially inferior because of race."

In a 1991 address to a conference of church social justice workers from throughout the United States, Bishop Francis described some of the developments leading up to *Brothers and Sisters to Us*. The pastoral came about, he explained, "as a result of a resolution presented to the [1976] Call to Action assembly by a coalition of Hispanic Americans, Native Americans, and African Americans. It was clear to that coalition that the Catholic Church in this country was not seen as particularly concerned about the prominent place racism held in both the Church and society. Furthermore, African Americans were viewing the Catholic Church more and more as a 'White person's church.' Too many incidents, too many pronouncements and far too much silence on the presence of racism in society and the Church gave credence to this attitude."

Bishop Francis said, "The Catholic Church is losing the brightest and the best of its young African and Hispanic Americans." Dissatisfaction "with the Church's response to racism" is at work in this development.

I might note here that Archbishop Lyke once called racism "not only a sin, but a sickness." He said in 1989 that racism in the United States is "a deep mental illness that throws the psychic center off balance."

Archbishop John Roach of St. Paul and Minneapolis said in a January 1991 pastoral letter that the conditions that result from racism are "morally offensive. They violate our most basic sense of what is right and just." Similarly, in Bishop Thomas Daily's first pastoral letter to the people of the Diocese of Brooklyn in December 1990, he said: "We are forced to conclude from what the Bible teaches us that antagonism and divisiveness within

the human family are the result of sinful free choice, totally contrary to the will of the Creator."

The same year, Bishop William Friend of Shreveport, La., cautioned in a pastoral letter that "no human person may be reduced to an object or used as a mere means. . . . No one may exploit another human person for the purpose of one's pleasure or advantage. This is an unconditional moral demand."

HUMAN DIGNITY

"All men and women are created in God's image; not just 'some' races and racial types, but 'all' bear the imprint of the Creator and are enlivened by the breath of his one Spirit," the U.S. bishops said in *Brothers and Sisters to Us*.

The bishops added that in the mystery of the Church "all men and women are brothers and sisters, all one in Christ, all bear the image of the eternal God." And the "Church has a duty to proclaim the truth about the human being as disclosed in the truth about Jesus Christ."

But what's the problem here? Isn't the Church already proclaiming this truth about the human being? Apparently the answer is both yes and no.

Archbishop Lyke said in 1989 that "we have done a poor job of reaching the hearts of our White sisters and brothers, and motivating them to respect the dignity and rights of minorities. We need to intensify such efforts."

Interestingly enough, it was only two years earlier that the U.S. Catholic Conference Administrative Board found it necessary to issue a statement on the membership of Catholics in the Ku Klux Klan. "We state unequivocally that Catholics who join the Ku Klux Klan or any organizations that actively promote racism act in violation of Catholic teaching," said the Administrative Board. The problem, the board explained, is that "the sin of racism defiles the image of God and degrades the sacred dignityof humankind."

It would be difficult to count the number of

times Pope John Paul II has spoken on the basic dignity of the human person. On December 4, 1993, he situated this concern precisely in the context of racism when he addressed U.S. bishops from California, Nevada, and Hawaii who were making their required "ad limina" visits to Rome. "Racism is an intolerable injustice by reason of the social conflicts which it provokes, but even more so by reason of the way in which it dishonors the inalienable dignity of all human beings, irrespective of their race or ethnic origin," the pope said.

But again, isn't the Church proclaiming this teaching already? Again the answer: yes, but no.

On such matters, "Catholic social teachings have been bold and uncompromising," the Black Catholic Clergy Caucus board of directors said in 1992. The sad problem, it added, is that these teachings "are all too often unknown, unpreached, untaught, and unbelieved."

DOCUMENTS CITED

U.S. Black Catholic Bishops, "What We Have Seen and Heard." *Origins*, Vol. 14 (Oct. 18, 1984), 273-287.

Black Catholic Clergy Caucus, "The Message After Los Angeles." *Origins*, Vol. 22 (June 4, 1992), 63-64.

Bowman, Sr. Thea, FSPA, "To Be Black and Catholic." *Origins*, Vol. 19 (July 6, 1989), 113-118.

"Cardinal Suspends Priest Who Founds African American Congregation," texts by Father George Stallings, Cardinal James Hickey and Auxiliary Bishop John Ricard. *Origins*, Vol. 19 (July 20, 1989), 153-157.

Daily, Bishop Thomas, "Created in the Image of God." *Origins*, Vol. 20 (Jan. 3, 1991), 488-492.

Ernst, Jerome, "Another Look at Rodney King." *Origins*, Vol. 22 (June 4, 1992), 64.

Francis, Bishop Joseph, "A Century of Social Teaching." *Origins*, Vol. 20 (March 14, 1991), 658-659.

Francis, Bishop Joseph, "Pastoral on Racism Called Church's Best-Kept Secret." *Origins*, Vol. 14 (Nov. 29, 1984), 393.

Friend, Bishop William, "That All May Be One." *Origins*, Vol. 20 (Aug. 16, 1990), 175-178. Gregory, Bishop Wilton, "African-American Catholics and the Summer of '89." *Origins*, Vol. 19 (Sept. 7, 1989), 225-231.

John Paul II, "African Sanctuary of Black Pain: Slavery's Roots." *Origins*, Vol. 21 (March 5, 1992), 632-633.

John Paul II, "Ad Limina" remarks to bishops from California, Nevada, and Hawaii. *Origins*, Vol. 23 (Jan. 13, 1994), 538-540.

Lyke, Bishop James (later archbishop), "Response to Father Stallings and Imani Temple." *Origins*, Vol. 19 (Sept. 7, 1989), 232-237.

National Black Catholic Congress, "The African American Family." *Origins*, Vol. 22 (Aug. 20, 1992), 189-203.

Pontifical Justice and Peace Commission (now, council), "The Church and Racism." *Origins*, Vol. 18 (Feb. 23, 1989), 613-626.

Roach, Archbishop John, "Social Justice: Reviving the Common Good." *Origins*, Vol. 20 (Feb. 14, 1991), 585-593.

"The Rodney King Verdict and Its Aftermath," texts by Cardinal Roger Mahony, Archbishop James Lyke, Bishop Walter Sullivan, Bishop John Sullivan, and Catholic Charities USA's Association of Directors and Administrators. *Origins*, Vol. 22 (May 21, 1992), 17-23.

Steib, Bishop J. Terry, "Africa's Influence on U.S. Catholics." *Origins*, Vol. 23 (April 28, 1994), 789-790.

U.S. Bishops, *Brothers and Sisters to Us.* *Origins*, Vol. 9 (Nov. 29, 1979), 381-389.

U.S. Bishops, "A Response: African American Evangelization and the National Black Catholic Pastoral Plan." *Origins*, Vol. 19 (Dec. 28, 1989), 485-492.

U.S. Catholic Conference, statement on Ku Klux Klan membership. *Origins*, Vol. 16 (April 9, 1987), 746.

CATHOLIC AFRICAN AMERICANS: A HISTORICAL SUMMARY

REV. CYPRIAN DAVIS, OSB

If the story of America is told with honesty and clarity, we must all recognize the role that Blacks have played in the growth of this country. At every turning point of American history, we come face to face with the Black man and Black woman.[1]

The history of Black Catholics in the United States closely parallels the history of the Catholic Church in the United States. Blacks were present at the foundation of the Catholic Church in America and present also in varying degrees as the Church spread throughout the land with new arrivals of immigrants. Black Catholics played a dynamic role in the growth and development of the Catholic Church in the South prior to the Civil War. Throughout the history of the Church in the United States, Black Catholics have offered

NEITHER SLAVERY NOR RACISM PREVENTED THE PURSUIT OF HOLINESS.

Catholicism both a challenge and a reproach. This history can be divided into five major periods: (a) Colonial Period, (b) Civil War Period, (c) Post Civil War Period, (d) World War I Period, and (e) Civil Rights Period.

COLONIAL PERIOD

The Spanish were the first to arrive in what is now the United States. Their first settlement, St. Augustine, was made in northern Florida in 1565. Except for the period from 1763 to 1784, Florida would remain the northern outpost for the Spanish Empire in the western hemisphere until 1821 when it became a United States territory. From the beginning Blacks, both slaves and freedmen from Spain or from Africa, were part of the colony. As the British settled the Carolinas and Georgia, they became the hostile neighbors to the Spanish colonists. The latter encouraged the slaves in these English colonies to escape. If they did so, they were promised freedom and refuge in the Spanish colony, provided they converted to the Catholic Faith. In 1738 an all-Black town, Gracia Real de Santa Teresa de Mose, was established for many of the freed slaves. Thus the first Black town in American history was a town of Black Catholics. In

1759 this fortified town sheltered sixty-seven inhabitants and a Franciscan priest. It was an armed settlement, for the males in the town were also part of the militia defending the Spanish colony. Unlike the English and Americans, the Spanish had no qualms in arming its Black inhabitants. In fact, by 1683 a militia of mulatto and Black soldiers had already been established in St. Augustine.[2]

The Spanish population evacuated Florida in 1763 and returned only in 1784. From that year until 1821 when the Spanish colony became a territory in the United States, Blacks, both slave and free, played an important role in Florida, as slaves and freedmen, as soldiers and artisans. By the end of the eighteenth century, over half of the population was Black and Catholic.[3] A Black Spanish-speaking population was likewise found in the Southwest. In 1781, settlers from Mexico founded the city that was to be known as Los Angeles. Of the eleven families that made up the original inhabitants, only two men were Spaniards; the rest were either mulattoes, mestizos, Negroes, or Indians. Thus over half were of African descent.[4]

Black Catholics were found as well in the French colony of Louisiana by the beginning of the eighteenth century. By the middle of that century, they far outnumbered the settlers.[5] The Code Noir that governed the life and behavior of the slaves mandated their baptism and religious instruction but it is uncertain how many were able to practice their religion in the back country of Louisiana. The baptismal registers in Mobile, Savannah, and Vincennes in Indiana all indicate the presence of Black Catholics. They were found in the French-speaking territories of St. Louis, St. Genevieve in Missouri, and in Kaskasia and Cahokia in Illinois.[6]

In 1785 John Carroll, soon to become America's first bishop, wrote the officials in Rome indicating the presence of three thousand Catholic slaves in Maryland, which represented 20 percent of the total Catholic population.[7] By the beginning of the nineteenth century, many of the Catholic families of Maryland had moved with their Catholic slaves to central Kentucky where they established a second English-speaking Catholic settlement.[8]

By the first quarter of the nineteenth century, the presence of a Black Catholic community is apparent. In 1824, Charles Nerinckx, the frontier Belgian missionary priest who founded the Sisters of Loretto in 1812, established a related community of three Black sisters who would serve as catechists for the slave community. Nerinckx himself, having been forced from office, died shortly thereafter. Those who succeeded him had little concern for Black sisters. The three were dismissed.[9] Five years later, a second community of Black sisters was begun in Baltimore. This community was composed of four Black Haitian women with Elizabeth Lange as superior. The religious life had been a dream for these four Black women already operating a school for Black children. The dream was made a reality through the initiative of Jacques Joubert, a French Sulpician and pastor for the Haitians who assembled every Sunday in the lower chapel of St. Mary's Seminary on Paca Street. Founded in 1829 and approved by Pope Gregory XVI in 1831, the Oblate Sisters of Providence became the nucleus for a Black Catholic community in that city. From the beginning they were educators at a time when Black children were generally neglected.[10]

Thirteen years after Black sisters appeared in Baltimore, two women, Creoles of color, began a religious community of Black sisters in New Orleans. Of the "Free People of Color"—men and women of mixed ancestry who were segregated and rejected by the White population because of their African ancestry—many of the women, noted for their beauty, formed non-legal alliances with well-to-do White men. The young Henriette Delille defied all the expectations of her milieu and determined with the help of Juliette Gaudin of Haitian parentage to found a community of Black sisters. After two unsuccessful attempts, in 1842 the Sisters of the Holy Family were finally established to teach, to nurse, and to serve the destitute among the Black population.

The existence of two religious communities of Black women in the period of slavery seems a miracle. In the final analysis, it is an argument for the spiritual vitality of the antebellum Black Catholic community, a community that was mature and autonomous enough to nurture religious vocations. Some of the sisters, in fact, even moved from slavery into the convent with their manumission papers.[11] In an age when most Whites assumed that Blacks were inferior and prone to sensuality, young Black women gave themselves to Christ in the service of the poorest and the most neglected. The general disdain for Blacks was often visited upon the Black sisters. An example of this bias is that the Sisters of the Holy Family could not appear on the streets of New Orleans in religious habit until 1872.[12]

Neither slavery nor racism prevented the pursuit of holiness. The cause for the canonization of Elizabeth Lange and Henriette Delille has already been begun. Another candidate for sainthood today is Pierre Toussaint, a Haitian who was brought to the United States in 1787 at the age of twenty-one by his owner, Jean Berard, and who became the sole support of Madame Berard when her husband died. Freed by his owner on her death bed, Pierre Toussaint, who had been trained as a hair dresser and who had as his clientele the aristocratic women of New York, eventually purchased the freedom of his sister and the woman whom he married. In his long life, Toussaint lived a life of selfless charity and service to others. Far from being poor, he was both a philanthropist and a social worker, rich in piety and good works. He died in 1853, acclaimed by his Protestant admirers as an authentic saint. His cause also has been introduced in New York.[13]

Like other Blacks in pre-Civil War America, Black Roman Catholics in Baltimore formed self-help groups. To date, the best documented self-help group is the Society of the Holy Family, a group of two hundred Black men and women who met weekly at the cathedral parish hall from 1843 to 1845 according to a record of their meetings kept by their White chaplain. This account reveals their piety, their almsgiving, and the instructions delivered by their chaplain.[14]

CIVIL WAR PERIOD

No issue divided the United States in its history as did the issue of slavery. It divided families, friends,

organizations, and Churches. It divided individuals within themselves. It marked Americans and African Americans alike, and the consequences of slavery still affect American society. For a long time Catholics in America paid scant attention to the involvement of the Church with slavery.

Many religious communities, like the Jesuits, the Vincentians, the Sulpicians, and the Dominicans, owned slaves. Congregations of sisters, like the Dominicans, the Ursulines, the Sisters of Charity, and the religious of the Sacred Heart, owned slaves. Contemplative nuns like the Carmelites were slave owners. Parish priests and bishops were slave owners. Some slaves were treated very well. Other slaves owned by Catholics were exploited worse than those owned by non-Catholic lay persons. Without exaggeration one can say that the Catholic Church in the South before the Civil War owed its physical and material development to the labor of men and women who were never paid for their services and were degraded and demeaned as persons. In the period before the Civil War, the Catholic Church in this country both wore the chains of slavery and wielded the whips of slave masters.

Some church leaders went so far as to justify slavery. Others sought to ameliorate it. Almost no Catholic leader in America took a public stand against it or joined the ranks of the Abolitionists until just before the Civil War. And in 1839 when Pope Gregory XVI condemned the slave trade in his papal brief *In Supremo Apostolatus*, Bishop John England of Charleston published a series of articles in his diocesan newspaper to deny that the pope was criticizing or condemning slavery as it existed in the United States.[15] Unfortunately, the American hierarchy sought to hide from the moral issue of slavery by insisting that the whole slavery debate was a political issue. In doing so, they appear before the bar of history as men who shirked their duty "to preach the word in season and out."

The Catholic press in general was opposed to the Abolitionists and supported the cause of slavery. Leading Catholic laymen, like James A. McMaster, editor of the *Freeman's Journal* of New York, and

John Mullaly, editor of the *Metropolitan Record,* also of New York, were outspoken supporters of slavery and White supremacy.[16] It was only in 1862 that Edward Purcell, editor of the *Catholic Telegraph* of Cincinnati, came out publicly for the emancipation of the slaves. His brother, John B. Purcell, the archbishop of Cincinnati, was one of the few bishops in America who publicly supported emancipation.[17]

POST-CIVIL WAR: 1865-1904

The Catholic Church in the United States faced a serious challenge after the Civil War in the several million freed slaves. In October 1866, the Second Plenary Council of Baltimore presented a remarkable show of unity in a country where most of the Churches had been divided over the slavery issue. Among the questions that Martin J. Spalding, the archbishop of Baltimore, wished addressed by the council was the need for concerted action to minister to the needs of the freed slaves. "Four million of these unfortunates are thrown on our Charity . . . a golden opportunity for reaping a harvest of souls, which neglected, may not return."[18]

With the approval of the Roman Curia, Spalding had proposed in the discussion document drawn up by the Curia that someone be appointed by the bishops to coordinate nationwide evangelization efforts for all African Americans. It was strongly suggested that this coordinator be a bishop. With few exceptions the assembled bishops greeted the suggestion with anger and dismay, seeing this as a derogation of their own episcopal jurisdiction. The opposition was so strident that Spalding seemingly never revealed that the idea, which had the enthusiastic support of the curia officials, was originally his idea. The bishops rejected the proposal of a national coordinator. It was finally agreed that the bishops would tend to the problem of Black Americans individually in their respective dioceses. The "golden opportunity" was lost.[19] The council's closing pastoral letter was marked by a remarkable lack of sensitivity.

> We could have wished . . . a more gradual system of emancipation could have been adopted, so

that they [the freed slaves] might have been in some measure prepared to make a better use of their freedom, than they are like to do now. Still the evils which must necessarily attend upon the sudden liberation of so large a multitude, with their peculiar dispositions and habits, only make the appeal to our Christian charity and zeal, presented by their forlorn condition, the more forcible and imperative.[20]

Partly as a result of the failure to realize his project for evangelization, Spalding arranged for the coming of the Mill Hill Fathers to the United States, a missionary society founded by Herbert Vaughan, future cardinal archbishop of Westminster. In 1871 four priests of the fledgling society arrived in Baltimore where Spalding gave them the African American parish church of St. Francis Xavier. Vaughan had insisted that the missionary society was to work exclusively for the evangelization of the Black population. He toured a large part of the South, noting with dismay the tremendous hostility of American Whites, including Catholics, towards Blacks.[21] In 1893, the Mill Hill Fathers in the United States separated from the parent body in England and became the Society of St. Joseph or the Josephites.[22]

The Third Plenary Council of Baltimore took place in 1884. At this council a system of annual collections for the evangelization of Indians and Blacks was instituted. To facilitate the distribution of the gathered funds, a commission was established made up of three bishops, one of whom was the archbishop of Baltimore, and a priest secretary.[23]

Despite the Catholic Church's traditional policy of encouraging a native clergy, despite the presence of African students in the Urban College in Rome attached to the Congregation of the Propaganda Fide, efforts to have an indigenous African American clergy met opposition and hostility from the U.S. bishops from the beginning. The Healy brothers, born into slavery in Georgia, the sons of an Irish-born slave holder, Michael Morris Healy, and his slave, Mary Eliza, became the first Black African American priests. Educated in the North and proteges of the two bishops of Boston, John

Fitzpatrick and John Williams, both James Augustine Healy, ordained in Paris in 1854, and Alexander Sherwood Healy, ordained in Rome in 1858, became priests of the Boston diocese. A third brother, Patrick Francis Healy, became a Jesuit and was ordained in Liege, Belgium, in 1864. Patrick became president of Georgetown University in 1874. The following year his brother, Alexander Sherwood, died. In the same year James Augustine became the second bishop of Portland, Maine, and the first Black Catholic bishop in American history.[24]

These men along with their siblings were exceptional. Although recognized as Black, with the exception of Patrick Healy who was accepted as White, and despite their birth as slaves, their experience in the Black community had been limited. Their home and careers had been within the clerical structure of New England. More typical of the Black experience was the fruitless attempts made by William Williams, a young Black man from Virginia, who was admitted into the Urban College in Rome in 1855 but who sought in vain for a U.S. bishop to adopt him. The bishops were convinced that a Black priest would not be acceptable in the United States. In 1862, Williams abandoned his studies in Rome and returned to the States. For many years he cherished the dream of being ordained, but his dreams were never realized.[25]

It was another ex-slave who became the first truly well-known Black priest in the United States. Born in 1854 on a plantation in rural Missouri, Augustus Tolton escaped into Illinois thanks to the resourcefulness of his mother, Martha Tolton, who crossed the Mississippi in a row boat with her three children. Finding it impossible to find a seminary for his studies for the priesthood, Augustus Tolton obtained a place in the Urban College in Rome thanks to the efforts of the Franciscan minister general. In 1886, he was ordained a priest in St. John Lateran in Rome and returned to a rousing welcome in Quincy, Ill. Assigned to a parish for the service of Black Catholics, Tolton soon experienced harassment and hostility from a neighboring priest. A man of simplicity and generosity, Tolton experienced the loneliness and the abandonment that many of the first

African American priests who came after him were to know. Moving to Chicago in 1889, he died there worn out in heart and body in 1897.[26]

Tolton died young, but his influence had been widespread. He played a role in the achievements of the African American community in the last decade of the nineteenth century. Perhaps the greatest contributions that Black Catholics made to the Catholic Church in the United States were the initiative and creativity of its laity. Black priests were few until the middle of the twentieth century. In fact, by the year 1950 only fifty-three Black men had been ordained to the priesthood for service in the United States.[27] It was the laity that began to assume responsibility for evangelization, recognition, and growth for the African American community in the Catholic Church. This began with a movement of which Tolton was a part in the last decade of the nineteenth century.

Between the years 1889 and 1894, Black Catholic laymen met in five congresses, the first in Washington, D.C., in 1889 and the last in Baltimore in 1894. The inspiration for these congresses came from a Black newspaper editor named Daniel Rudd who had been born in Bardstown, Ky., in 1854. Rudd had begun publishing his weekly Black Catholic newspaper in Cincinnati around 1888. In his newspaper and later in his many lectures throughout the country, he spoke of the Catholic Church as the means by which racial discrimination would be overcome. The Church was seen as the great uplifter of all races, including African Americans. He predicted that as the Church came to be seen as the advocate and champion of African Americans, there would be a massive conversion of African Americans to the Catholic Church. He proposed that Black Catholics meet in a congress so that Black Protestants and White Catholics could see the extent and the strength of the Black Catholic community. For him the Black Catholic community was to be a "leaven" for both Blacks and Whites.[28]

The members of these congresses were delegated by their parishes. Many of them were local leaders. Their concerns as Catholic leaders were not confined simply to church affairs but addressed problems of social justice and racial discrimination in society. In their closing statements they expressed their love and devotion for the Church but at the same time professed their determination to see that the Church would remain truly Catholic and rid itself of the sinful aspects of racial prejudice. They charged the Church to take responsibility for the education of Black children by opening trade schools and business schools. In their own way they began to devise a body of Black Catholic thought in which they saw the Church in terms of their own historical roots in Africa and in the African saints. Above all they elaborated a theological analysis of Church and vocation that helped forge a unique Catholic community.[29]

Another initiative taken by the Black Catholic laity was an appeal to the Holy See regarding the condition of Black Catholics. As early as 1853, a New York Black woman, Harriet Thompson, wrote to Pope Pius IX describing the racial insensitivity of Archbishop John Hughes and the lack of Catholic schooling for Black Catholic children. Twenty-six persons signed their names with hers.[30] Thirty-one years later in 1884 members of the Black Catholic Congress Grievance Committee announced plans to take to Rome the results of their own investigation into the practices of racism in the United States Church.[31] About nine years later, a Belgian priest, Albert Anciaux, SSJ, who worked among Black Catholics in Arkansas, Virginia, and in various other assignments, wrote a passionate report on the Miserable Condition of Black Catholics in America. This little work, marked "confidential," was addressed to the Holy Father and was sent to the Roman Curia.[32]

In 1904, Cardinal Girolamo Maria Gotti, prefect of the Congregation of the Propaganda Fide, wrote to the apostolic delegate, Archbishop Diomede Falconio, OFM, asking him to pass on to Cardinal James Gibbons a letter expressing concern regarding the way Black Catholics were treated in certain dioceses in the country. Gibbons was to be instructed to confer with the nation's archbishops in order to devise a plan to stop this sort of treatment.[33] What information caused Cardinal Gotti to write

this rather peremptory letter remains unclear. More than likely the Roman Curia had been the recipient of many complaints regarding racial discrimination within the United States Church. What is interesting is that it was a very conservative Roman Curia which took up the question of Black Catholics in an unfriendly Church.

PROTEST AND INITIATIVE; PROJECTS AND PROGRAMS

Between 1904 and 1924 three parties came together in confrontation and collaboration around the issue of Catholicism in the United States and the African American. One was Roman, the second was American, and the third was African American. The Roman factor was the effort made by the Roman Curia under the direction of Cardinal Gaetano De Lai of the Consistorial Congregation to deal with the evangelization of African Americans. Central to their activities was the conviction that the U.S. bishops had paid little attention to the Black members of their flock. The Roman response was to begin a policy of direct intervention.

Faced with the unspoken accusation of apathy, the U.S. bishops responded with bureaucratic measures and sought to stave off substantive measures such as creating a Black priesthood. In the midst of these forces Black Catholics were mobilized by an extraordinary lay leader, unusual by his foresight, courage, and faith.

The apostolic delegation files reveal correspondence between Cardinal De Lai and Cardinal William van Rossum, CSSR of the Congregation of the Propaganda Fide, and Archbishop Giovanni Bonzano, the apostolic delegate. The two curial officials sought information on the population growth of Black Catholics, the quality of the ministry afforded them, and the best means for increasing the number of Black priests. De Lai took it upon himself to obtain independent reports from European observers regarding the situation of Black Catholics in the southern United States. He likewise sought out long-term strategies for their evangelization. Both De Lai and van Rossum were convinced that the U.S. bishops had not made a concerted effort to evangelize the Black community. Interestingly enough the ghost of the Second Plenary Council of 1866 appeared in the correspondence of the two curial cardinals. Rome was never quite satisfied that the U.S. bishops had not accepted the idea of a national ordinary for the evangelization of African Americans. They saw such a personage as crucial to any efficient coordination of ministry programs for Blacks in the United States.[34]

The U.S. bishops, however, thought to respond to the 1804 letter of Cardinal Gotti by establishing the Catholic Board of Negro Missions with a New York priest, John E. Burke, as director. Burke, when asked by Bonzano for his suggestions regarding the evangelization of African Americans, responded with a carefully detailed report. For Burke, two solutions were of paramount importance: the need for Black priests and the need for Black parish churches in order to remove Black Catholics from church buildings where they were regularly segregated in the balcony or in some other corner within the church. Included with his report was another report from a Josephite priest, John Albert, proposing the creation of a permanent diaconate, that is married Black men ordained to the office of deacon and prepared to officiate in those parishes in the South where the White priest could not always be present.[35]

WORLD WAR I PERIOD

Thomas Wyatt Turner, a Black Catholic lay leader of the first half of the twentieth century, is, like Daniel Rudd, one of the most important leaders in the history of Black Catholics in this country. Like Rudd he was born in Virginia in 1877 and grew up in humble surroundings, the son of a share cropper. Unlike Rudd, he was a university professor and an intellectual. Like Rudd, he was a loyal Catholic but much more realistic, perhaps, in his assessment of what the Church could do for African Americans.

Already involved in the struggle for civil rights, Turner was thrust into the forefront of the Black Catholic cause during the First World War when he and other leading Black Catholics appealed to

Cardinal Gibbons concerning the lack of care given to Black Catholic soldiers. At the time, various religious organizations provided services and amenities to the troops. The White section of the YMCA aided White Protestant troops, the Black YMCA aided the Black Protestant troops, and the Knights of Columbus, all White, aided the White Catholic troops. No one was responsible for aiding the Black Catholic troops. Through the efforts of Turner and his committee, this lack of assistance was remedied.

By the end of the war the group had developed into the Committee Against the Extension of Race Prejudice in the Catholic Church and would later become the Committee for the Advancement of Colored Catholics. Turner was relentless in his pursuit of justice for African American Catholics within the Catholic Church. He believed in organizations, strategies, and programs. He was convinced that the Catholic Church had to be truly universal to be true to itself. It was also his conviction that Blacks must be the leaders in the advancement of their own cause and that they must speak for themselves. By 1924, the Committee for the Advancement of Colored Catholics had become the Federated Colored Catholics, the organizational successor of the Black Catholic lay congresses of the 1890s. In 1919, Turner had written Archbishop Bonzano, the apostolic delegate, sending him a copy of the letter which he had sent earlier to the U.S. bishops regarding the thoughts and desires of the African American Catholic community. These concerns centered around the lack of encouragement of vocations for Black Catholic priests; the lack of educational opportunity for Black Catholic children who most often had no access to secondary Catholic education; the failure of Catholic University, a pontifical university in the nation's capital, to admit Black students; and finally the fact that Blacks were not represented in the various Catholic organizations that advised the hierarchy or influenced policy.[36]

The work of Turner was complicated by the attitudes of two prominent White priests, William Markoe, SJ, and John LaFarge, SJ, who were champions of justice for Black Americans and were his collaborators in the Federated Colored Catholics. In the end, a violent quarrel broke out between the Jesuit priests and Turner,[37] resulting in a split in the Federated Colored Catholics in 1932. On the other hand, the influence of Father LaFarge helped establish the Catholic Interracial Councils, which would become the preferred means for the interracial apostolate within the Catholic Church. This was a change of strategy. Put succinctly, Turner believed in action-oriented organized protest; LaFarge believed in the value of discussion and interracial meetings. In the end Turner's hard-hitting, project-oriented, Black-led organization would be the direction of the future in the Civil Rights period.[38]

CIVIL RIGHTS AND BLACK CONSCIOUSNESS

By 1930 there were about 200,000 Black Catholics out of a total Black population of 11,000,000 or more. The majority of Black Catholics were found in the dioceses of Baltimore; New Orleans; Lafayette, La.; New York; and Brooklyn.[39] By 1930 a seminary for Black candidates for the priesthood had been established in Bay St. Louis, Miss., by the Society of the Divine Word, but its first ordination class of four Black priests would not take place until 1934. In 1930 there were only two black diocesan priests in the United States and one Black Josephite.[40]

By 1930 a third community of Black sisters, the Franciscan Handmaids of Mary—founded in 1916 in Savannah, Georgia, by Ignatius Lissner, SMA, and Mother Theodore Williams to meet a threat that White sisters might be prohibited by law from teaching Black students—had established itself in Harlem where they served an economically deprived Black population with a soup kitchen, a day nursery, and teaching in the parochial school.[41] In 1931 Xavier University in New Orleans under the auspices of the Sisters of the Blessed Sacrament became the first Black Catholic university.

In the next fifty years there was an unprecedented growth and transformation in the Black Catholic community in America. In 1940 the number of

Black Catholics in the nation was about 300,000 out of a Black population of 12,000,000.[42] In 1975 the number of Black Catholics in the nation was 917,000 out of a Black population of 23,000,000.[43] In 1940 the dioceses and archdioceses with the largest number of Black Catholics were Lafayette, La.; New Orleans; Baltimore; Washington; Chicago; New York; and Brooklyn. In 1975, Lafayette still had the largest number of Black Catholics, Chicago was second, then New Orleans, Washington, and New York.

Within three decades the number of Black Catholics had more than doubled. The centers of Black Catholicism had increased. Louisiana and southern Maryland and the District of Columbia had remained Catholic centers, but other urban areas had an increase in the number of Black Catholics as well. Only in the 1950s, however, did the number of Black priests begin to increase. By 1958, one hundred Black priests had been ordained since 1854 when James Augustine Healy was ordained. In 1966 Harold Perry, SVD, became the second Black bishop in American history when he was made auxiliary bishop of New Orleans. The Black Catholic population grew in numbers especially in the North for two reasons: (1) the increase of Catholic education for Black children and the encouragement of non-Catholic Black parents to receive instruction, and (2) the general perception that Catholicism was friendly to Blacks. By 1947 bishops like Joseph Ritter of St. Louis and Patrick O'Boyle of Washington, D.C., had publicly ended racial segregation in the Catholic schools of their respective dioceses. It was only in 1958, however, that the United States bishops took an unequivocal stand against racism and segregation.[44]

It was ten years later in the turmoil following the assassination of Martin Luther King Jr. that Black priests, summoned to Detroit for the meeting of the Catholic Clergy Conference for Interracial Justice, met together beforehand and formed a caucus on April 16-17, 1968. This meeting of Black Catholic priests was the turning point for Catholic involvement in the Civil Rights Movement. The assembled Black clergy drew up a statement addressed to the

U.S. bishops. Militant in tone and incisive in its demands, the statement listed grievances that Black Catholics had experienced in the Catholic Church in the United States. By forming themselves into a permanent body known as the National Black Catholic Clergy Caucus, Black priests became a catalyst for change on behalf of the Black Catholic community. That same year Black women religious formed the National Black Sisters Conference. Subsequently, the National Black Catholic Seminarians Association and the Black Catholic Lay Congress were established. Finally, in 1971 the National Office of Black Catholics, headquartered in Washington, D.C., was established.

Despite the mood of confrontation, despite the angry rhetoric and the equally angry responses, despite the friction between Catholics of European ethnic background and African Americans, the Catholic Church in the United States underwent a momentous change within a short span of time. There were four major signs of this change. First, the National Office of Black Catholics moved from an outpost situation to a liaison office—a move from confrontation activity to consultation services. From the ranks of the Black Catholic clergy emerged twelve Black bishops. After the episcopal ordination of Harold Perry in 1966, Joseph Howze was ordained bishop in 1973 and the first ordinary of the diocese of Biloxi in 1977. Within fifteen years, from 1973 to 1988, eleven Black bishops were ordained, including two ordinaries, Archbishop Eugene Marino and Archbishop James Lyke of Atlanta. Almost overnight the Black clergy had become a voice within the establishment.

The third sign of an enormous change was the publication of a pastoral letter by the U.S. bishops, branding racism as a sin and calling for an end to racism within the society and also within the Church. The pastoral letter, *Brothers and Sisters to Us*, appeared in 1979. Finally, in 1987 the Bishops' Committee on African American Catholics and the Secretariat for African American Catholics were established. By this time almost every diocese with a substantial number of Black Catholics had established an office for Black Catholics on the local church level. The Black Catholic community is now structurally an integral part of the Catholic Church in the United States.

In the last decade of the twentieth century, Black Catholics now number almost two million. As a religious body Black Catholics are as large as if not larger than some of the Black Protestant Churches. They are as numerous as the membership of some mainline Protestant Churches. In 1984 the Black bishops published a pastoral letter on evangelization, *What We Have Seen and Heard,* proclaiming that African American Catholics were no longer a missionary field but mature Christians with the responsibility of evangelizing themselves and others. The letter clearly acknowledged the gifts of Black people that were to be used in building up the Church. Since that date two Black Catholic Congresses have been celebrated—the first since the five at the end of the last century—one in 1987 and the second in 1992.

Today the Black Catholic community is a strong, vibrant, and colorful component of the Church in the United States. The music and the liturgical celebrations of African American Catholics with their African motifs and idioms have added a different dimension to the traditional Roman Catholic music and liturgy in this country. The development of workshops, symposia, and the establishment of a summer institute of Black Catholic Studies at Xavier University in New Orleans point to the rise of a new crop of Black Catholic theologians and scholars prepared to dialogue with their counterparts in the Black Protestant traditions and prepared to enrich the common heritage of Roman Catholics and African Americans. Despite the residue of racism that still clings to many American institutions including the Catholic Church in the United States, despite the tragedy of the schism of the gifted and brilliant preachers George Stallings and Bruce Greening, who brought into existence the Imani Temple, and despite the myriad of social problems that beset the African American community in many urban settings, the Black Catholic community has enabled the Catholic Church in America to enter the next millennium as truly Catholic and integrally American.

NOTES

1. *What We Have Seen and Heard: A Pastoral Letter on Evangelization from the Black Bishops of the United States* (Cincinnati: St. Anthony Messenger Press, 1984), 17.

2. For information regarding the Black community at St. Augustine, see Jane Landers, "Black Society in Spanish St. Augustine, 1784-1821," dissertation (University of Florida, 1988).

3. Ibid.

4. David Weber, ed., *Foreigners in Their Native Land: Historical Roots of the Mexican Americans*, 6th edition (Albuquerque: University of New Mexico Press, 1981), 34-35.

5. According to Gwendolyn Midlo Hall, *Africans in Colonial Louisiana: The Development of Afro-Creole Culture in the Eighteenth Century* (Baton Rouge: Louisiana State University, 1992), in 1746 there were 1,700 White settlers in all of the Louisiana territory compared with 4,730 Black slaves in the same area.

6. See Cyprian Davis, OSB, *The History of Black Catholics in the United States* (New York: Crossroad, 1990), 72-85. See also Carl Ekberg, *Colonial Ste. Genevieve: An Adventure on the Mississippi Frontier* (Gerald, Mo.: The Patrice Press, 1985), and Charles Balesi, *The Time of the French in the Heart of North America: 1673-1818* (Chicago: Alliance Franaise Chicago, 1992), 246-53.

7. Thomas Hanley, ed., *The John Carroll Papers* (Notre Dame: University of Notre Dame Press, 1976), vol. 1, 179-82.

8. See Davis, *History of Black Catholics*, 28-39.

9. Davis, *History*, 98-99.

10. Sr. M. Reginald Gerdes, OSP, "To Educate and Evangelize: Black Catholic Schools of the Oblate Sisters of Providence, 1828-1880," *U.S. Catholic Historian* vol. 7 (1988), 183-99.

11. The archives of the Oblate Sisters of Providence have some of the manumission records of women who moved from slavery into the convent.

12. See Davis, *History*, 105-109.

13. See Ellen Tarry, *The Other Toussaint: A Post-Revolutionary Black* (Boston: St. Paul Editions, 1981).

14. Sulpician Archives (Baltimore) (RG 42, box 2).

15. "Letters to the Hon. John Forsyth, on the Subject of Domestic Slavery; to which are Prefixed Copies, in Latin and English, of the Pope's Apostolic Letter Concerning the African Slave Trade, with Some Introductory Remarks, etc.," in *The Works of the Right Rev. John England, First Bishop of Charleston, Collected and Arranged under the Advice and Direction of His Immediate Successor, the Right Rev. Ignatius Aloysius Reynolds, and Printed for Him in Five Volumes* (Baltimore: John Murphy, 1849), vol. 3, 106-91.

16. See Madeleine Hooke Rice, *American Catholic Opinion in the Slavery Controversy* (New York: Columbia University Press, 1944), 124-26.

17. See "Father Purcell's Stand in Behalf of Emancipation of the Slaves, April 8, 1863," in *Documents of American Catholic History*, ed. John Tracy Ellis (Wilmington, Del.: Michael Glazier, 1987), vol. 1, 378-83.

18. From a letter of Spalding to Archbishop McGloskey of New York, October 9, 1865. Edward Misch, "The American Bishops and the Negro from the Civil War to the Third Plenary Council of Baltimore, 1865-1884," Ph.D. dissertation (Rome: Pontifical Gregorian University, 1968), 182.

19. Minutes of the extraordinary session of the Second Plenary Council of Baltimore, 39A-D5 (Archdiocese of Baltimore Archives). For a discussion of this session, see Davis, *History*, 118-20.

20. *The National Pastorals of the American Hierarchy, 1792–1919*, ed. Peter Guilday (Washington, D.C.: National Catholic Welfare Council, 1923), 220-21.

21. Stephen J. Ochs, *Desegregating the Altar: The Josephites and the Struggle for Black Priests, 1871-1960* (Baton Rouge: Louisiana State University, 1990), 43-45.

22. Ibid., 82-85.

23. Misch, "The American Bishops and the Negro," 315-24; 329-37.

24. Davis, *History*, 146-52.

25. Ochs, *Desegregating the Altar*, 29-31.

26. Davis, *History*, 152-62.

27. See Ochs, *Desegregating the Altar*, Appendix A, listing all Black priests from 1854 to 1960, 456-60.

28. Davis, *History*, 164-75.

29. Ibid., 175-94. See also *Three Catholic Afro-American Congresses* (Cincinnati: American Catholic Tribune, 1893), reprint (New York: Arno Press, 1978).

30. Davis, *History*, 94-97.

31. Ibid., 190. See article in the *New York Sun* for June 29, 1894, "The Treatment of Colored Catholics by the Church."

32. This little book is found in the Apostolic Delegate files in the Vatican Library, Del. ap. U.S.A. I, 160b/1 (1911-14/1919), *Condizione dei negri*. It is also in the Josephite Archives in Baltimore, Joseph Anciaux, *De Miserabili Conditione Catholicorum Nigrorum in America* (Namur: Typis Jac. Godenne, n.d.).

33. Davis, *History*, 195.

34. For most of this material, see Davis, *History*, 198-205.

35. Ibid., 200-204.

36. For information regarding Turner, see Marilyn Nickels, *Black Catholic Protest and the Federated Colored Catholics, 1917-1933: Three Perspectives on Racial Justice* (New York: Garland Publishing, 1988).

37. Ibid., 91-135.

38. For the interracial councils, see Martin A. Zielinski, "Working For Interracial Justice: The Catholic Interracial Council of New York, 1934-1964," *U.S. Catholic Historian* vol. 7 (1988), 233-60.

39. See the figures in John T. Gillard, *The Catholic Church and the American Negro* (Baltimore: St. Joseph's Society Press, 1929), 47-54.

40. For the establishment of the seminary for training Black priests by the Society of the Divine Word, see *Ochs, Desegregating the Altar*, 246-76. For the diocesan priests, see Albert Foley, *God's Men of Color: The Colored Catholic Priests of the United States 1854-1954* (New York: Farrar, Straus and Co., 1955).

41. See Davis, *History*, 240-42.

42. See John T. Gillard, *Colored Catholics in the United States* (Baltimore: The Josephite Press, 1941), 14-15.

43. George Shuster, SSJ, and Robert M. Kearns, SSJ, *Statistical Profile of Black Catholics* (Washington, D.C.: Josephite Pastoral Center, 1976), 18-19, 34.

44. "The American Catholic Bishops and Racism, November 14, 1958," *Documents of American Catholic History*, vol. 2, 646-52.

ST. CHARLES BORROMEO PARISH: A NEW YORK SUCCESS STORY

REV. JOSEPH FITZPATRICK, SJ

When the word Harlem is mentioned in conversation, it generally evokes images of a Black metropolis "evolved within the womb of a city," a unique cosmopolitan milieu throbbing with the sights and sounds of Black folks from the north and south, from Africa, from the West Indies, and from the Caribbean and South America. Within Harlem there are numerous centers and institutions of creative life that speak to the needs of all people. The parish of St. Charles Borromeo is one of them. Already beyond its centenary, it is the central Catholic parish in Harlem, the seat of the vicar, the site of a flourishing parochial school, and the center of religious and social activity.

Established in 1888 as a parish for Irish immigrants, St. Charles Borromeo had become "the Cathedral of Harlem" by the turn of the century. Following World War I, African Americans seeking better jobs and better opportunities moved into Harlem. In spite of the prejudice and hostility of the White population, large numbers of African Americans

were attracted to the Catholic Church, which offered, among other things, a strong school system. Inspired by the deep faith of the African American parishioners, Fr. O'Donnell, the pastor, instituted convert classes and invited the Sisters of the Blessed Sacrament to staff the school, which had previously been maintained by the Christian Brothers and the Sisters of Charity. By 1930, St.

Charles Borromeo, now predominantly African American, could still boast that it was the Cathedral of Harlem.

STATUS AND CHALLENGES OF THE PAST

There is a saying around the parish that if you checked every Black Catholic in the New York metropolitan area, probably one third of them would have had some association with St. Charles. Various writers have pointed out that most Black leaders in the area have been trained in Catholic schools, some of them at St. Charles Borromeo. The parish is one of the old institutions by which most people identify the Catholic presence.

Probably the best way to describe the parish of St. Charles Borromeo would be "creative adaptation in the midst of great social and religious challenges." The survival of the parish is, in itself, something of a miracle. But more important than its survival is the remarkable way in which the clergy and parishioners developed a church of great vitality in the presence of enormous challenges. Perhaps this creative adaptation by the parish family of St. Charles Borromeo can serve as an example to other parishes facing rapid and radical change. St. Charles Borromeo successfully faced the challenges of transition from an all-White parish to a predominantly African American parish; the controversy of whether to emphasize sacramentalism or social action; the challenge of the Civil Rights Movement; and the tragedy of destruction of the church by fire.

Acutely aware of the need for a broader social outreach, the parishioners consistently pushed the pastors to become more involved in social concerns. Perhaps it was the sheer dynamism of the Civil Rights Movement of the 1960s embraced so enthusiastically by the parish's indigenous leadership coupled with the efforts of Msgr. Drew that moved the parish to address two of the most pressing social issues of the neighborhood: the need for better housing and the need for a community center. Sustained and encouraged by his parish leadership,

Msgr. Drew worked with the parish and local diocesan officials as well as other agencies to establish the Kennedy Center, a focal point for the community. Their vision for better housing also came to life with the establishment of new low-cost housing projects within the parish boundaries; fittingly enough, one of the projects was named the Drew Hamilton Houses.

Since education had always been perceived by the African American community as the vehicle for advancement, it is not surprising that the parishioners turned their attention to the need for a new school. Their vision was enthusiastically shared by the new pastor, Fr. Scanlon, and a new school was completed in 1963. Deeply committed to the larger issues of the time, the St. Charles Borromeo parish family embraced the liturgical changes after Vatican II and became an active participant in the Ministerial Interfaith Association of Harlem. A Montessori School to provide specialized education was also established. The school proved to successfully train many teachers in the Montessori method.

The creative tensions of the Civil Rights Movement continued to test the resolve of the African American community and at the same time solidify the **intransigence** of many White Americans. The subsequent social upheavals in Watts, Detroit, and Newark as well as in Washington, D.C. after the death of Martin Luther King Jr. were telling examples of this tension. It was in the midst of such tension that the vicariate of Harlem was established to give voice to all the parishes in Harlem. The first Black priest to become a pastor of St. Charles Borromeo, Fr. Harold Salmon, was appointed vicar. His broad understanding of the problems and his forthright leadership were very much appreciated by the vicariate parishioners, as well as by the family of St. Charles Borromeo. A devastating fire destroyed the church in 1968. Once again, the force behind the move to rebuild the church was the solidarity and commitment of the African American family, which saw its efforts rewarded in 1972. With new, expanded facilities, the parish continued to grow and became a vital center for religious life and community action programs. It was with a deep sense of pride that the parish community of St. Charles Borromeo welcomed Pope John Paul II into their midst in 1979. At that time, too, the parish was blessed with the pastorate of Fr. Emerson Moore, who was later ordained as the first Black bishop of Harlem. Bishop Moore continued the involvement of the parish in the activities of social action and the vicariate concerns. A senior citizens' housing complex was clearly the result of the bishop's and the parishioners' efforts.

STATUS AND CHALLENGES OF THE PRESENT

With understandable pride in their past accomplishments, the parish with its current pastor, Msgr. Wallace Harris, continues to be a vital force for both the Catholic and the larger Harlem community. The center of parish life is the liturgy, and the beautifully restored church is the perfect setting for such worship. On entering the church, one is immediately drawn to the altar, the banners, and the rich symbols reflecting an African American motif. The liturgy of the Mass is enhanced by the adult Gospel choir. In addition, the parish is blessed with an enthusiastic children's choir, which is an integral part of the liturgy. The parish takes great pride in its efforts to include all family members. Several examples of that effort are seen in such events as honoring the birthdays of all those more than 60 years old. These honored elders are presented with flowers and a birthday cake at a social gathering after all the Masses. Bearing in mind the ancient African proverb: *"It takes a whole village to raise a child,"* the parish during Black History Month dedicates the first Sunday to honoring mothers and sisters, the second Sunday to fathers and brothers, the third Sunday to sons and daughters, and the fourth Sunday to the extended family. An active RCIA program with fifteen adults and a CCD program with about thirty children is the primary focus for instructing those drawn to the faith.

Tithing is the major source of financial support for the parish. The success of that method of support reflects the serious commitment and determination of the parish family to keep the parish self-sustaining. Two sections of the parish council, the financial committee and the advisory committee, work closely with the pastor in designing and carrying out parish activities. The Holy Name Society and the Rosary Society also play an integral role in the parish's social action programs.

The most important response to the larger community is through the St. Vincent de Paul Society, which not only oversees the weekly distribution of food for the needy but also collaborates with the Partnership of the Homeless. When a homeless family is relocated to a dwelling within the parish, the members of the St. Vincent de Paul Society visit them to assist their adjustment to their new home and welcome them to the community.

The parish community of St. Charles Borromeo is particularly sensitive to the need for activities. The vicariate, in fact, recently concluded a very successful series of parenting workshops for single parents, touching the lives of more than 150 young mothers.

The school also plays an important role in the life of the parish. Started in 1924, the school was initially staffed by the Sisters of Charity and the LaSalle Christian Brothers until 1926 when the Sisters of the Blessed Sacrament accepted the responsibility for its future growth. The new school (built in 1963) with a staff of sixteen teachers has 530 students enrolled in grades kindergarten through eight. One impressive feature of the lay staff is their continuous service to St. Charles Borromeo. The student body is 30 percent Catholic. All students take a full course in religion and attend weekly Mass. A great deal of attention is given to connecting the students to the grandeur and beauty of their African American culture. That so many of the school's graduates are readily accepted into the private high schools of the area is due to St. Charles Borromeo's academic excellence—an excellence also recognized by the Middle States Association, which has fully accredited St. Charles Borromeo. Due to the continued support of a committee of dedicated parents, teachers, and administrators, morale is high and has a positive influence on the students.

In September 1994, the school embarked upon single-gender classes in its first four grades. The objective of this educational arrangement is to provide an opportunity for more direct attention to the needs of young African American boys. The program, based on the acclaimed Project 2000, is designed to provide strong male role models for these young boys to enhance their developing positive self-image and self respect. The project, which invites adult African American men to spend a minimum of three hours a week interacting with the young boys in a classroom, has enjoyed success in other cities and is expected to be successful at St. Charles.

CHALLENGES OF THE FUTURE

The parish community of St. Charles Borromeo now faces the coming of the twenty-first century, which will surely provide new challenges and opportunities for growth. The parish's capacity to adapt successfully is well established and gives everyone confidence that it will meet the future as creatively as it has met the past. New York City itself is now a predominantly minority city, with 83 percent of children in the entire school system either Hispanic, Asian, or Black. St. Charles Borromeo School already plays a significant role in educating these future adults, who will have the potential for leadership in the Catholic Church and in the world. As a sacramentally rich parish, St. Charles Borromeo will continue to be deeply involved in the community, facing the inevitable challenges of fulfilling the Gospel mandate of feeding the hungry, clothing the naked, and giving shelter to the homeless. Given the dedication and spiritual depths of their African American Catholic community, St. Charles Borromeo will remain, what it has always been, a sign of hope for the future.

ST. AGNES-OUR LADY OF FATIMA PARISH: A CLEVELAND SUCCESS STORY

SR. ELEACE KING

St. Agnes, located on Cleveland's east side, was established in 1893 to serve German and Irish immigrants, but towards the middle of the twentieth century, new immigrants from Puerto Rico moved to the area. Responding to the needs of Spanish-speaking Catholics, the diocese established Our Lady of Fatima parish, under the pastoral leadership of the Missionary Servants of the Most Holy Trinity (Trinitarians). When a further residential shift occurred with the increase of African American parishioners in the 1960s and 1970s, St. Agnes and Our Lady of Fatima were merged, and a new facility was created under the patronage of St. Agnes-Our Lady of Fatima.

The late archbishop, James Lyke, when he served as auxiliary bishop of Cleveland and vicar for East Cleveland, envisioned fewer churches with dynamic, sizable, self-supporting communities. St. Agnes-Our Lady of Fatima is the prototype of that vision, as it is in the process of being merged with a larger African American parish.

The parish is located in the Hough area of Cleveland, which has undergone several changes since the social upheavals of the 1960s. Among the more significant and hopeful changes is the movement of young, professional families back to the area, attracted by a city program offering residential lots at an attractive price. The increase of these new single-family dwellings augurs well for the Hough district, as well as for the churches and parishes that serve the residents.

Proud of its racial diversity of Blacks, Whites, and Hispanics, there is a strong sense of neighborhood and belonging in the area served by St. Agnes-Our Lady of Fatima. It is truly an urban mix: teenagers engaged in football at a park that once housed the Cleveland Indians, streets resounding with the laughter of children at play, and elderly and parents sitting on their front porches chatting and greeting passersby. The parish family of St. Agnes-Our Lady of Fatima takes pride in being a pastoral and spiritual force in this dynamic neighborhood that has had its share of urban challenges and opportunities.

Like many inner-city parishes, St. Agnes-Our Lady of Fatima is experiencing a steady growth; to the more than 250 parishioners, twenty-six were added last Easter, and among that number were sixteen teenagers who bring their youthful enthusiasm to a vibrant parish.

WORSHIP AND FELLOWSHIP

The parish community celebrates its Sunday liturgy at 10:00 A.M. The hallmark of the liturgy is its participation focused on the central idea that this is a worshiping community bound by love of the eucharist and one other. To that end, the liturgy involves both song and dance. The entrance procession, for example, is generally followed by the liturgical dance performed by a youth group. Songs are accompanied by an organ, as well as drums and an electric guitar. The church decorations reflect the African American presence, with statues and pictures depicting African American saints and spirituality.

Following the liturgy, the congregation gathers at the parish hall to share food and fellowship. It is not uncommon for many parishioners to spend a good portion of the afternoon in conversation.

Clearly, it is this sense of the freedom to be oneself, the feeling of acceptance and the feeling of "we-ness" that accounts for the sustained growth of the parish family. "This is a family here," said a sixty-eight-year-old gentleman who recently converted to Catholicism. "Everybody likes it; you won't find anybody who says different. You're just accepted for who you are. Everybody is welcomed here."

"THIS IS A FAMILY HERE.... YOU'RE JUST ACCEPTED FOR WHO YOU ARE."

There is genuine pride, too, in the way that St. Agnes-Our Lady of Fatima is held in high esteem by the larger community. The many social and cultural outreach programs have provided services to Hough residents regardless of religious affiliation. The focus of these varied activities is the parish community center, a licensed Catholic Charities Agency established in 1971. Headstart, tutoring, GED classes, and day care are ongoing educational and social programs of the center. The parish Hunger Center, with its daily lunch program for children, and food pantry program for needy families are generously staffed by volunteers from the parish. Once a week the parish family reaches out to and invites the needy to a hot meal prepared and served in the parish hall.

YOUTH MINISTRY

Youth activities abound at St. Agnes-Our Lady of Fatima. The parish family plays an active role in the lives of its youth. In addition to the two athletics programs for different age groups, there is a genuine concern for the academic performance of the students. Students who have demonstrated academic excellence are recognized at the annual awards banquet, which honors those who have served the church and the community by their academics as well as their athletic prowess.

Clearly one unique outreach program fostered by the parish is the "rectory program" in which the pastor allows chronically truant young men who are at least eighteen years old to live at the rectory while they complete high school. The security, stability, and structure of the rectory have helped several young men reach their goal.

However, the parish family of St. Agnes-Our Lady of Fatima takes greatest pride in the religious dimension of its youth outreach. Religious instruction for pre-teens is part of the Dismissal Bible School, conducted as part of the eucharistic liturgy. Before the first reading, the teens are given a blessing and, accompanied by their teachers, are dismissed from the congregation for religious instruction. The fourth Sunday of each month is Youth Sunday. At this liturgy, young people serve as lectors, commentators, ushers, and eucharistic ministers and sing in the choir. While only high school seniors are eucharistic ministers, younger students may serve in other capacities. The celebration is open to non-Catholics as well and over the years has been a catalyst for sixteen teenagers being baptized during the Easter season. The following scenario is not uncommon: one seventeen-year-old who was recently baptized first came to St. Agnes-Our Lady of Fatima to join the basketball team. One day he came early to shoot some baskets and found other teens doing homework in the "loft," which was once the gallery of the old church. Finding companionship and a good atmosphere for study, he began to come regularly and eventually joined the youth group. As he tells the story, he went to practice early one Sunday so he could go to Mass. After this he went early every Sunday. Ultimately he joined the youth RCIA program and converted to Catholicism.

NEW PROGRAMS

One of the exciting aspects of St. Agnes-Our Lady of Fatima parish is its focus on the future, always attentive to that which is possible for growth. Just recently the ministry coordinator—similar to a parish council—investigated three new projects: parenting classes for new mothers, integrating the spiritual dynamics of motherhood and the practical aspects of caring for infants; a ministry of support for addictive parishioners; and "Cookies from the Hood," involving volunteer adults and young people in an economic development project.

The parishioners can take rightful pride in their community involvement. As a founding member of "Neighbors Organized Around Housing," the parish is also a member of Hough Area Apartments in Progress and respected by the diocesan pastoral council and the Black advisory board.

Whatever the future may hold for St. Agnes-Our Lady of Fatima, the parishioners today clearly demonstrate that it is a faith-filled African American community touching the lives around them with gentleness, compassion, and love. Perhaps one of the elders said it best: "Just tell folks that we're just a bunch of ordinary people who love and care for each other."

ST. SABINA PARISH: A CHICAGO SUCCESS STORY

SR. ELEACE KING

St. Sabina parish, located on Chicago's south side, is unique in a variety of ways. Established in 1916 to serve a primarily Irish congregation, today this Gothic-style church is a self-sufficient, thriving African American Catholic community that boasts 2,000 members and a school of 500 students in grades kindergarten through eight.

Situated in the Auburn-Gresham area of Chicago, St. Sabina parish represents a cross-section of stable neighborhoods in an urban setting with Hispanic families coming from Mexico, the Caribbean, and South America, as well as indigenous Africans from Ghana and Nigeria. The majority of parishioners are African American. Because the members of this strongly focused African American parish consider themselves *"doers of the Word,"* the parish has been successful in curbing some of the problems traditionally associated with urban neighborhoods, such as drugs and urban blight.

The inspiring Gothic structure serves the parish well, for the growing community of worshipers clearly needs the space. The decor of the church speaks to African American culture. A large mural of the risen Christ is clearly a captivating universal image; the painting titled "For God So Loved the World" depicts a Black Christ with his arms outstretched and standing between the hands of God the Father. The side altar is dedicated to Rev. Martin Luther King Jr. and his vision of a world free of the burden of racism. A banner hanging over the bust of Dr. King quotes the words from Genesis: *"Your brother's blood cries out to me from the soil."*

St. Sabina is blessed with a cadre of strong, committed, Gospel-minded lay leaders who give of their time and effort in the ministry of service in many areas, but three in particular: social outreach and youth ministry, worship, and education.

SOCIAL OUTREACH AND YOUTH MINISTRY

Evidence of the parish's outreach can be seen in its two youth centers: the Rev. Martin Luther King Jr. Center and the Ark, both of which provide teens and young adults with age-appropriate social, athletic, and academic activities. During the past year alone, some 6,000 young people utilized the services of the centers. The Ark houses a portion of St. Sabina's School; however, this spacious building with a gym, fitness room, and meeting rooms is available for the neighborhood. In fact, the Ark is the home base for the "Young Warriors," a group of young people who have committed themselves and their gifts to improving their neighborhoods by demonstrating a young Christian lifestyle.

St. Sabina's efforts at social outreach have also attracted nationwide attention. Recently the parish was featured on the ABC news magazine, *Day One*. Over the years the parish has protested billboards advertising alcohol, cigarettes, and drug paraphernalia. Now the parish is joining other groups to rid the community of guns. Such sustained efforts are due in large measure to the serious commitment of dedicated African American lay leaders and pastoral leaders willing to take the risk. It is worth noting that the rectory of St. Sabina's is also the home of two young men—one is the adopted twenty-five-year-old son of pastor Michael Pfleger and the other is a local college senior who serves as a parish lay minister.

Another means of parish outreach is the general assistance program, which tries to meet the broader needs of the neighborhood by providing food, furniture,

clothing, and financial assistance. Obviously, such a program could not function without the constant dedication and commitment of the parish community.

WORSHIP

The parish family of St. Sabina's gathers at three liturgies on most weekends, a vigil Mass at 5:00 P.M. on Saturday and two Masses on Sunday at 8:30 and 11:15 A.M. Each of the liturgies radiates the joy and gratitude of the people of God called to worship and service. The liturgies are enhanced by parish choirs. But formal worship is not the only ingredient that attracts others to St. Sabina; there is the sharing of faith and the deepening of spirituality that comes from their gatherings to share the Bible.

The parish has recently begun a group called "new members—new believers." This three-month program is designed for Catholics joining St. Sabina's and for non-Catholics interested in learning more about the Church, some of whom intend to convert. Bible-based classes acquaint the newcomers with Sacred Scripture and prayer leading the participants to a deeper personal relationship with Jesus. At the end of the three-month program, newcomers enter into the second phase of membership, "watch-care." At this time, neophytes are placed in the care of other parishioners who serve as personal, psychological, and spiritual support for several months. Those who are catechumens or candidates for Catholicism also participate in The Rite of Christian Initiation for Adults (RCIA), which is recommended by the National Conference of Catholic Bishops.

> MEMBERS OF THIS STRONGLY FOCUSED AFRICAN AMERICAN PARISH CONSIDER THEMSELVES "DOERS OF THE WORD."

EDUCATION AND FINANCE

The parish family of St. Sabina takes its mission of Catholic education very seriously. The students in the school are well grounded in the traditional "three R's" but they are equally well grounded in their faith. St. Sabina Academy has a strong African American male and female presence in its principal, faculty, and staff who are acutely aware of their responsibility to educate the children for the world of the twenty-first century. Religious instruction, for example, is part of the daily curriculum whether the student is Catholic or not. Each Sunday the 8:30 Mass is primarily for children of the parish.

Interestingly enough, the 11:15 Mass is referred to as the "teaching Mass" because all in attendance are encouraged to bring their Bibles. During the Bible-based sermon, questions are addressed and notes are taken for further clarification and discussion.

How does a distinctly inner-city parish manage to sustain all of these social institutions and educational programs? Clearly, the parish community takes seriously the Lord's commands, *"From what you have, take an offering for the Lord,"* and *"Bring the whole tithe into the temple."* St. Sabina's is a tithing parish. This profound understanding of the scriptural command to give back to the Lord a portion of his gifts is bolstered by a sense of ownership. St. Sabina's is not some outside entity to which parishioners belong; this faith-filled, inspired African American Catholic community sees itself as St. Sabina.

CONCLUSION

While St. Sabina's may be best known for its social justice activity, those who view the parish from that perspective miss the reason for the activism—the faith foundation of the Church. St. Sabina is a community of faith. It is faith that inspires the commentator to greet the congregation with *"Good morning, Church"* and the celebrant to intone *"Pray, Church."*

Keenly aware that they are part of the body of Christ and that when one member suffers, they all suffer, parishioners routinely describe their work in the parish as "body ministry." A community steeped in Scripture and committed to being *"doers of the Word,"* both priest and people thank God for the blessing that each has in the other. Clearly this African American parish family lives up to its motto: *"See how they love one another."*

ST. AUGUSTINE'S PARISH: A WASHINGTON, D.C. SUCCESS STORY

REV. RICHARD BURTON

In a recent workshop titled *Pastoring in African American Parishes VII*, Dr. Andrew Billingsley from the University of Maryland observed that the institution of slavery was ended not so much by presidential decree as by the slaves themselves. Even though the African people brought to the Americas were enslaved, they nevertheless knew who they were and from whence they came and generated the internal resources to free themselves.

At the same workshop, the noted Black historian, Cyprian Davis, OSB, emphasized this important point in a different way. "Black leadership," he said, "came from the Black laity." A cogent example of this was Thomas Wyatt Turner, who organized the "Committee for the Advancement of Colored Catholics," which later became the "Federated Colored Catholics." This group of courageous, dedicated Catholic laity pressed for Black clergy and for Black admittance to The Catholic University and, in general, kept Rome and the American bishops aware of racism in the Church.

The existence of the Black lay congresses was largely due to the inspiration, perspiration, and preparation of Black Catholic laity. Spearheaded by such men as Charles H. Butler, the first of these five historic congresses was held at St. Augustine Church, Washington, D.C., in January 1889. Thus, the ministry of this parish is closely intertwined with lay initiative.

As far back as 1800, Black Catholics in the Washington area were single-minded in their efforts to form their own parish. Interestingly enough, it was President Abraham Lincoln himself who held a strawberry festival on the grounds of the White House to raise money for the establishment of a Black parish, St. Matthew's. St. Matthew's flourished as did the school, St. Martin de Porres, which opened in 1858. It is from these roots that the "first St. Augustine's" came to be. Canonically established as a parish in 1865, the cornerstone of what was to be a truly grand Gothic-style church was not laid until July 14, 1874. Seating some twelve hundred people, the beauty and grandeur of the church were symbolic of Black Catholic pride and

THE MINISTRY OF THIS PARISH IS CLOSELY INTERTWINED WITH LAY INITIATIVE.

clearly remained so until 1947 when the property was sold.

A new St. Augustine's, with school, rectory, and convent, was erected the following year, and the parish thrived. In September 1961, however, the faithful of St. Augustine's were merged with the parish community of St. Paul. Understandably disturbed by what they perceived as diocesan hubris, the community of St. Augustine, with characteristic commitment to their faith, effected a smooth merger with St. Paul's, creating a St. Paul/St. Augustine parish. The merger was clearly fortuitous, for in a few years a revitalized parish was called St. Augustine's.

A conscious effort has been made by the parish to preserve its history; to that end, the parish has established an archive room and hired an archivist to oversee the historic materials.

St. Augustine's today is in many ways a model parish of committed, dynamic Catholic lay leadership. The parish's focus on liturgical worship, parish ministry, and social outreach provides ample opportunity for lay involvement and leadership.

One notes immediately the care and attention given to the various liturgical celebrations, which effectively involve the parish family and encourage a broad range of lay participation. The ministry of the word is enhanced by the ministry of song rendered by an outstanding Gospel choir numbering more than seventy-five members. A young adult choir also provides ample opportunities for parish involvement.

St. Augustine's is rich in multigenerational parish ministries. There is an outreach to the young, to families, to single parents, and to the elderly. Family retreats and marriage encounters are also important aspects of ministry. The after-school African American cultural program addresses the needs of the pre-teens with the Aesop-Nia Program. A very successful RCIA program, directed to adults and children, has been a valuable training ground for lay leadership. Indeed, each of the ministries is spearheaded by a strong, committed group of lay people. The social ministry of St. Augustine's is under the direction of a full-time outreach minister. Over the years, the parish has been the home base for such dynamic organizations as the Young Christian Workers, which, for a period of five or six years, played a major role in expanding Catholic social action. The parish was also the spiritual home to Friendship House, an organization whose efforts were directed to building sensitivity between diverse social groups. Out of these organizations emerged a strong cadre of African American leaders who together with their pastors were indefatigable in their efforts to combat racism. The integration of that powerful women's parish group, the Sodality Union of Washington, and the integration of the Catholic Youth Organization were clearly the combined efforts of lay and parochial leadership.

The history of St. Augustine represents lay empowerment at its best. Dynamic Catholic men and women have reorganized the compelling need to share their faith and their vision of what is means to be truly Black and truly Catholic. Perhaps it is also safe to suggest that the pastors who have served at St. Augustine's over the years, men like Olds, Mudd, Dillard, Kemp, and Bouchard, have in some measure found their source of inspiration and drive for social justice in the lives and examples of those intrepid Black lay leaders like Thomas Wyatt Turner, who organized the Federated Colored Catholics, and Charles H. Butler, who was instrumental in convening the first Black Catholic Lay Congress.

Stories of St. Augustine's involvement in the neighborhood, in the marketplace, and in world affairs abound. These accounts are a tribute to the zeal and commitment of a long line of African American lay leaders, their pastors, and their flocks who labored so diligently to preserve St. Augustine's—the Capital's oldest Black Catholic Church.

AFRICAN AMERICAN PROFILES FROM THE GENERAL SOCIAL SURVEYS, 1972-1990

DR. CHE FU LEE
REV. RAYMOND H. POTVIN

African Americans—the largest and most visible minority group in America numbering some 30 million and representing 12 percent of the nation's population—are often the most cited group in statistical profiles.[1] Unfortunately, the tendency among social scientists and others who "study" African Americans is to treat the group as a monolithic entity, whereas African Americans are perhaps the most diverse group in the American racial and ethnic mosaic.

Sadly enough, however, there are disproportionate numbers of African Americans below the official poverty level, and their plight is chronicled regularly. But that is only part of the reality, for there is scant attention paid to the non-poor but not affluent and the affluent African American. Increasingly there is the accepted conclusion that within-group differences among African Americans have increased particularly during the decades of the 1970s and 1980s. The life

chances of better educated, middle-class African Americans have improved, while the urban poor African Americans have been left behind and become more isolated socially and economically.[2]

There are two comprehensive and readily accessible publications by the Population Reference Bureau, Inc. of Washington, D.C., which summarize the characteristics of African Americans: "Black America in the 1980s" by John Reed[3] and "African Americans in the 1990s" by William O'Hare, et al.[4]

The following analysis will focus on the diversity of sociodemographic characteristics reflecting differences in socioeconomic strata among African Americans.

Although selected characteristics of Black Americans will be introduced briefly at the beginning of this chapter, statistical details available elsewhere generally will not be repeated. Rather, the present analysis will focus on the diversity of sociodemographic characteristics reflecting differences in socioeconomic strata among African Americans. As is well known, the economically disadvantaged are overrepresented among Black Americans and statistical aggregation of the group as a whole tends to understate the disprivileged conditions of poor Blacks while neglecting the true profile of the Black non-poor. Moreover, nearly half of the African Americans in the 1990s were born after the 1960s, the era of great social awakening and legislative reforms with respect to civil rights. To be useful as a policy guide, any narratives of the contemporary African American profile must take into account the diversity within this subpopulation, especially between the "truly disadvantaged" (Wilson's term) and other African Americans.

Based on cumulative data of annual surveys—General Social Surveys (GSS)—over the decades of the 1970s and 1980s,[5] this research construct profiles of the Black urban poor, the non-poor but not affluent, and the affluent. A relatively small percentage of Black Americans (less than 10 percent) residing in rural places will also be described. The GSS data, relative to census-type national data, are most useful for our purposes in that the survey questionnaires cover a broad spectrum of opinions and attitudes in addition to general sociodemographic variables.

This chapter is organized into the following sections: overall demographic profile, rural/urban and poor/non-poor, income and wage earners for urban and rural families, changing family characteristics, human capital, political participation and interracial sentiment, and religion and race. A summary is included at the end of the chapter.

OVERALL DEMOGRAPHIC PROFILE

The first census of the new republic taken in 1790 enumerated a total population of 3.9 million, one in five of African origin. In the early decades of this century the representation of African Americans declined to one in ten because of the surge of European immigration. As the waves of European immigration subsided after the 1930s, the proportion of Black Americans in the total American population recovered. It is now about one in eight Americans or 30 of the 250 million.

Until the first decade of this century African Americans were found predominantly in the South. With the declining agricultural economy of the South and the labor demand of the industrial North during World War II, Black Americans moved in large numbers away from the South. By 1960, Black Americans living in the South accounted for slightly more than half of all African Americans. This proportion has remained fairly stable, given a reverse trend of migration from the North to the South which began in the 1970s. Presently, 53 percent of African Americans live in the southern states, 19 percent live in the northeast, 19 percent in the midwestern states, and 9 percent in the West.

Although twentieth-century rural-urban migration led to the regional dispersion of African Americans, racial segregation between Black and White Americans' residences remained part and parcel of the urbanization process. African Americans' residences are greatly concentrated in metropolitan areas—84 percent in 1990—and of those African Americans found in metropolitan areas, the great majority live in central cities. On the other hand, one-third of metropolitan Whites have their residence in central cities and two-thirds in the suburbs. Though it appeared that a trend of increasing suburbanization for Black residences occurred during the decades of the 1970s and 1980s, closer analysis revealed that this so-called Black suburbanization was due largely to the spill-over of inner-city Black neighborhoods across the city borders, rather than to any substantial movement of inner-city Blacks to the middle-class suburban neighborhoods.[6]

In 1990, there were 20 U.S. cities with 150,000 or more Blacks, amounting to 9 million or 30 percent of all Black Americans (Table 1; Figure 1). This urban concentration of the Black population has been accompanied by a precipitous decline in the rural proportion of African Americans. Before the

Table 1: U.S. Cities with Black Populations of 150,000 or Greater, 1990

Black Rank	Overall Rank	City, State	Total Population (in thousands)	Black Population (in thousands)	Percent Black
1	1	New York, NY	7,322.6	2,102.5	29
2	3	Chicago, IL	2,783.7	1,087.7	39
3	7	Detroit, MI	1,028.0	777.9	76
4	5	Philadelphia, PA	1,585.6	631.9	40
5	2	Los Angeles, CA	3,485.4	487.7	14
6	4	Houston, TX	1,630.6	458.0	28
7	13	Baltimore, MD	736.0	435.8	59
8	19	Washington, DC	606.9	399.6	66
9	18	Memphis, TN	610.3	334.7	55
10	25	New Orleans, LA	496.9	307.7	62
11	8	Dallas, TX	1,006.9	297.0	30
12	36	Atlanta, GA	394.0	264.3	67
13	24	Cleveland, OH	505.6	235.4	47
14	17	Milwaukee, WI	628.1	191.3	31
15	34	St. Louis, MO	396.7	188.4	48
16	60	Birmingham, AL	266.0	168.3	63
17	12	Indianapolis, IN	742.0	165.6	22
18	15	Jacksonville, FL	673.0	163.9	24
19	39	Oakland, CA	372.2	163.3	44
20	56	Newark, NJ	275.2	160.9	59

Source: Bureau of the Census, 1991. Unpublished data from 1990 Census.

turn of this century, more than 80 percent of Black Americans were found in rural areas. By 1980, the rural percentage was reduced to 15 percent (compared with 29 percent for Whites). It was estimated to be lower than 10 percent in 1990.

The Black population has a younger age structure than that of Whites—a median age of 28 compared with a median age of 34 for Whites. The younger age structure of African Americans is attributed to a higher fertility rate. The average number of children born per Black woman (the total fertility rate) was estimated at 2.4 compared with 1.8 per White woman in 1990. This difference of 30 to 40 percent in the total fertility rates between Blacks and Whites has remained fairly stable over the past few decades. This is not surprising given the remarkably parallel trends of fertility between Blacks and Whites, namely a rise in the number of births during the 1940s and 1950s and the subsequent decline in the later 1960s. The higher fertility of Black Americans leads to a higher rate of natural increase (births in excess of deaths) relative to that of White Americans. With a younger age structure, more Blacks will be entering childbearing age in the future, and thus the relatively higher rate of natural increase of Black Americans is expected to continue well into the twenty-first century even if Black fertility should become equal to that of Whites. In other words, the proportional representation of African Americans is expected to grow in the foreseeable future, especially among the younger school-aged children and young adults who will be entering the labor force.

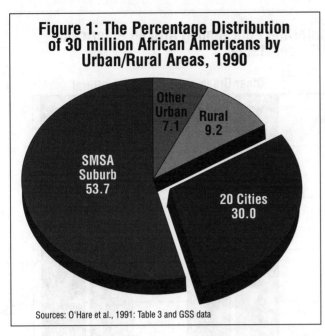

Figure 1: The Percentage Distribution of 30 million African Americans by Urban/Rural Areas, 1990

Other Urban 7.1
Rural 9.2
SMSA Suburb 53.7
20 Cities 30.0

Sources: O'Hare et al., 1991: Table 3 and GSS data

Fertility behavior is but one aspect of family life that differs substantially among economic strata for Black Americans. For example, the age and marital status of mothers who enter the stage of childbirth vary considerably by level of education and of earned income; consequently, the proportions of Black children to adults were very unevenly distributed among

different types of Black households. It is important therefore in any discussion of the Black population to specify and control for socioeconomic diversity.

RURAL/URBAN AND POOR/NON-POOR

African Americans are three to four times more likely than Whites to be poor. According to the Census Bureau's definition of the poverty line (an income three times the cost of an "economy food plan," adjusted for family size and the inflation factor), the percentage of Black families falling below the poverty line has fluctuated around 30 percent over the past three decades, while that of White families has leveled off at 10 percent or so (Figure 2). If the borderline poor (income at 125 percent of the poverty line) are included in our category, given the fact that family poverty is subject to short-term changes in members' employment status, the percentage of poor Black families can reach as high as 40 percent.

The high level of poverty for African Americans has been consistently borne out by estimates based

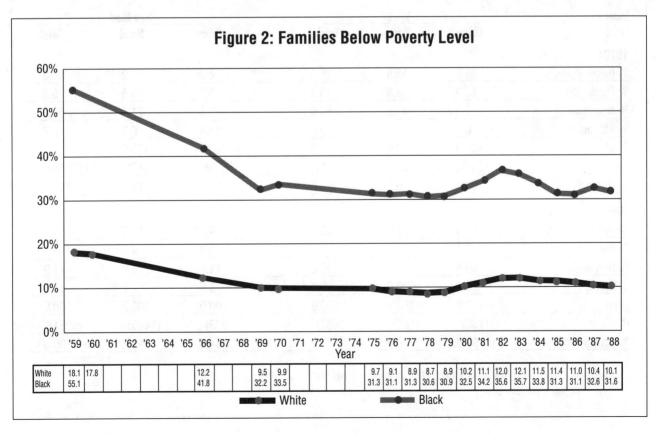

Figure 2: Families Below Poverty Level

	'59	'60	'61	'62	'63	'64	'65	'66	'67	'68	'69	'70	'71	'72	'73	'74	'75	'76	'77	'78	'79	'80	'81	'82	'83	'84	'85	'86	'87	'88
White	18.1	17.8						12.2			9.5	9.9					9.7	9.1	8.9	8.7	8.9	10.2	11.1	12.0	12.1	11.5	11.4	11.0	10.4	10.1
Black	55.1							41.8			32.2	33.5					31.3	31.1	31.3	30.6	30.9	32.5	34.2	35.6	35.7	33.8	31.3	31.1	32.6	31.6

White ●——● Black ●——●

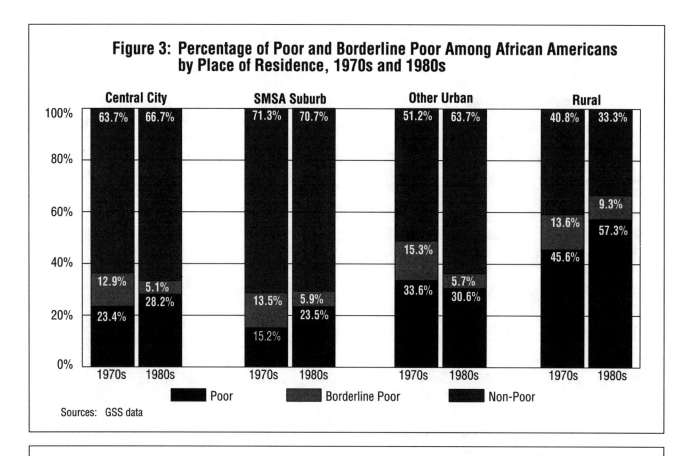

Figure 3: Percentage of Poor and Borderline Poor Among African Americans by Place of Residence, 1970s and 1980s

Sources: GSS data

Table 2: Level of Income by Race and Residence

Income Level	Black			Non-Black		
	Urban	Rural	Total	Urban	Rural	Total
1970s						
% Below Poverty	24.6	45.6	26.6	6.2	11.2	7.2
% Borderline	13.6	13.6	13.6	5.7	8.8	6.3
% Non-poor	55.3	40.8	54.0	69.6	71.4	69.8
% Affluent*	6.4	0.0	5.8	18.4	8.5	16.7
Total	100.0	100.0	100.0	100.0	100.0	
(N)	(1231)	(125)	(1356)	(8649)	(2019)	(10668)
% Urban/Rural	90.8	9.2	100.0	81.1	18.9	100.0
1980s						
% Below Poverty	27.9	57.3	30.3	9.6	13.2	10.1
% Borderline	5.4	9.3	5.7	3.4	4.2	3.5
% Non-poor	60.8	33.3	58.6	71.4	74.9	71.9
% Affluent*	5.8	0.0	5.4	15.6	7.7	14.5
Total	100.0	100.0	100.0	100.0	100.0	100.0
(N)	(1732)	(150)	(1882)	(7848)	(1403)	(9251)
% Urban/Rural	92.0	8.0	100.0	84.8	15.2	100.0

Source: GSS, 1972–1990. The 1970s = 1972–1980; the 1980s = 1981–1990.

*Family income $50,000 or more.

on the GSS data as shown in Figure 3 for the 1970s and the 1980s. This consistency justifies our use of the GSS survey data for constructing various profiles for Black Americans of different socioeconomic situations, namely the poor and non-poor, in the analyses that follow.

As shown earlier, in 1990, about 84 percent of the 30 million African Americans lived in metropolitan areas. About half of the other 16 percent were living in nonmetropolitan rural areas and the other half in nonmetropolitan urban areas.

While only 8 percent (about 2.4 million) of the Black population resided in rural areas, poverty was especially prevalent among them—59 percent during the 1970s and 67 percent during the 1980s were estimated as poor or borderline poor. Because of this high ratio, two out of three rural Blacks living in poverty compared with one in five for rural Whites, the rural Black population will be described separately in the subsequent analysis. Since Blacks in nonmetropolitan urban areas have only a slightly higher poverty rate than Blacks in metropolitan areas, these were combined into one urban category for the analysis. To explore the special characteristics, if any, of the upper-class affluent Black Americans, those with family incomes of $50,000 and higher (in 1986 dollars) will be selected for special analysis. The GSS data indicate about 5 to 6 percent of urban Black families fall into this category, but none or nearly none were found in rural areas. The percentage distribution of urban Black families by economic status, namely the poor, non-poor, and affluent, are presented and compared with that of non-Blacks, the White majority and other ethnic minorities in Table 2, for the 1970s and the 1980s.

URBAN FAMILIES: INCOME AND WAGE EARNERS

In order to see the gaps between the urban poor, non-poor, and the affluent in real dollars for Africans and other Americans, the average family incomes were computed from the GSS data for the 1970s and 1980s (Table 3). Since respondents were asked also the total number of earners in the household, it is possible to derive an average income per earner for the urban poor households, the non-poor households, and the affluent households. During the 1970s, the average family income for urban poor African Americans was $7,432 (standardized in terms of 1986 dollars), and the average number of earners in the family was less than one (0.97). During the same period, urban non-poor Black families had an average income of $23,344 with 1.52 earners on the average, about three times the income of the poor. Affluent urban Black families had again three times ($73,625) the income of the non-poor, with 2.57 earners on the average.

In terms of average earnings, then, the gaps were substantial. The urban poor Black earners made on the average $7,662 a year in the 1970s; their urban non-poor counterparts, $15,358; and the urban affluent, $28,648. The U.S. economy, during the 1970s and 1980s, was subject to inflation followed by a recession in the late 1980s. Except for urban affluent Black earners, who earned $31,641 on average in the 1980s, an increase of $2,993 from the 1970s, both non-poor and poor urban Black income improved hardly at all. In spite of the increase in average income per earner among urban affluent Black families from the 1970s to the 1980s, the average number of earners per family declined and their average family

THE LIFE CHANCES OF BETTER EDUCATED, MIDDLE-CLASS AFRICAN AMERICANS HAVE IMPROVED, WHILE THE URBAN POOR AFRICAN AMERICANS HAVE BECOME MORE ISOLATED SOCIALLY AND ECONOMICALLY.

Table 3: Mean Family Income (1986 Dollars) by Race, 1970s and 1980s

	Urban Poor	Urban Non-Poor	Urban Affluent	Rural
1970s Black				
Total	$7,432	$24,344	$73,635	$13,105
No. Earners	.97	1.52	2.57	1.40
No. Persons	3.68	3.14	4.43	3.66
Avg./Earner	$7,667	$15,358	$28,648	$9,361
Avg./Person	$2,020	$7,434	$16,620	$3,581
(N)	(422)	(629)	(76)	(119)
1970s Non-Black				
Total	$6,860	$26,448	$75,008	$25,806
No. Earners	.85	1.50	2.17	1.49
No. Persons	2.94	2.98	3.63	3.12
Avg./Earner	$8,071	$17,632	$34,566	$17,319
Avg./Person	$2,333	$8,875	$20,663	$8,271
(N)	(937)	(5660)	(1489)	(1884)
1980s Black				
Total	$8,424	$23,180	$70,243	$10,215
No. Earners	1.03	1.51	2.22	1.12
No. Persons	2.97	2.72	3.36	3.32
Avg./Earner	$8,179	$15,351	$31,641	$9,121
Avg./Person	$2,836	$8,522	$20,906	$3,077
(N)	(686)	(926)	(86)	(147)
1980s Non-Black				
Total	$20,239	$25,597	$81,568	$23,552
No. Earners	1.32	1.46	2.14	1.35
No. Persons	2.66	2.60	3.13	2.69
Avg./Earner	$15,333	$17,532	$38,116	$17,446
Avg./Person	$7,609	$9,845	$26,060	$8,755
(N)	(2086)	(5199)	(1061)	(1450)

income also declined, from $73,625 to $70,243. For urban poor Blacks, the average number of earners per family increased slightly, from 0.97 in the 1970s to 1.03 in the 1980s and this accounted for an increase in average family income of $1,000. Urban non-poor Black families remained at the same income and earner levels during the two decades.

It is interesting to note that, given the smaller family size and fewer number of earners in the families of non-Black urban poor, their average family income was lower even than that of the Black poor in the 1970s. However, the non-Black urban poor fared much better in the 1980s than in the 1970s, both in terms of average number of earners (1.32 vs. 0.85) and average income per earner ($15,333 vs. $8,071). Like the Black urban non-poor, their non-Black counterparts remained at approximately the same level in terms of earners and average income in the 1980s as in the 1970s. Among non-Black affluent families, the average family income rose from $75,008 to $81,568. During the decade of the 1980s, the non-Black affluent and the non-Black urban poor improved their economic status, but

none of the Black groups experienced much change in spite of inflation.

RURAL FAMILIES: INCOME AND WAGE EARNERS

Also presented in Table 3 are the income data for the rural Black and non-Black families. The data do not distinguish the poor and non-poor because, as explained previously, the rural Black sample is relatively small and the great majority of rural Blacks are poor. Average family income, even if the non-poor were to be included, was only slightly higher than that of urban poor Black families. Furthermore, their economic situation further deteriorated from the 1970s to the 1980s. Compared with rural non-Blacks, the rural Black family income was just half or less on average.

In terms of average income per earner, rural Blacks were at a level about 1.5 times that of the urban poor in the 1970s and nearly as low as the urban poor in the 1980s ($3,077 vs. $2,836). As

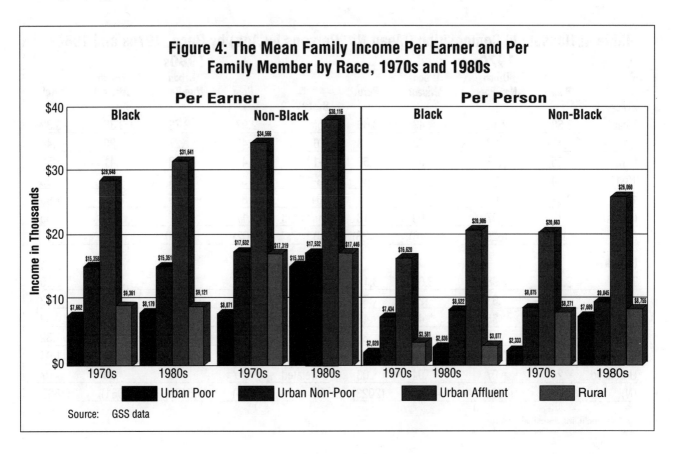

Figure 4: The Mean Family Income Per Earner and Per Family Member by Race, 1970s and 1980s

Source: GSS data

seen in Table 3, rural Black average earnings per earner were closer to the urban poor, while those of rural non-Blacks were more like their urban non-poor counterparts.

Figure 4 shows the average earnings per earner and average income per person in the household for each of the above economic classes. The gaps in family income together with differences in the average household size led to even greater disparities in average income per person. Among African Americans, income per person as a member of a poor household was about one-eighth of the counterpart of an affluent household and one-third to a quarter of that of a non-poor household.

The household size of the urban poor was slightly larger than the urban non-poor, but no larger than that of the urban affluent (Table 4). However, the poor households were younger, characterized by having more children under 18 years of age, especially those under 6, than the non-poor and the affluent.

To facilitate a visual comparison, the data in Table 4 on the average number of persons by age per household by different economic statuses for the 1970s and 1980s are presented graphically in Figure 5. The general trend for all groups from the 1970s to the 1980s was a further reduction of the household size. This reduction is attributable to a continued decline in the rate of childbirth, as well as the changing characteristics of American families—marital status and living arrangement—which will be discussed next. Nonetheless, the different household composition of the various economic strata has contributed to the disproportionate distribution of children found in households below the poverty line, especially for African American children. As shown in Figure 6, the number of Black children in poverty exceeded 40 percent in the 1970s and increased to some extent during the 1980s.

CHANGING FAMILY CHARACTERISTICS

Since 1960 the trend toward marrying later or not at all has been characteristic of both Blacks and other Americans. This trend, however, was especially

Table 4: Household Composition (Mean No. Persons by Age) by Race, 1970s and 1980s

	1970s					1980s			
	Poor	Urban Non-Poor	Urban Affluent	Rural		Poor	Urban Non-Poor	Urban Affluent	Rural
BLACK					**BLACK**				
Total*	3.68	3.14	4.43	3.66	Total*	2.97	2.72	3.36	3.32
< 6	.47	.37	.38	.28	< 6	.40	.27	.26	.44
6-12	.65	.43	.63	.50	6-12	.43	.33	.41	.56
13-17	.54	.32	.62	.54	13-17	.34	.24	.27	.35
18+	2.01	2.02	2.80	2.34	18+	1.81	1.89	2.43	1.96
Unrelated	.17	.07	.03	.13	Unrelated	.17	.07	.04	.05
(N)	(494)	(629)	(76)	(128)	(N)	(902)	(926)	(86)	(171)
NON-BLACK					**NON-BLACK**				
Total*	2.94	2.98	3.63	3.12	Total*	2.66	2.60	3.13	2.69
< 6	.35	.31	.23	.30	< 6	.26	.24	.18	.23
6-12	.41	.35	.47	.41	6-12	.31	.25	.31	.32
13-17	.33	.28	.49	.33	13-17	.20	.21	.31	.32
18+	1.84	2.03	2.44	2.08	18+	1.88	1.90	2.32	1.94
Unrelated	.28	.07	.04	.03	Unrelated	.20	.12	.04	.07
(N)	(1097)	(5660)	(1489)	(2023)	(N)	(3285)	(5199)	(1061)	(1803)

*Not including unrelated person

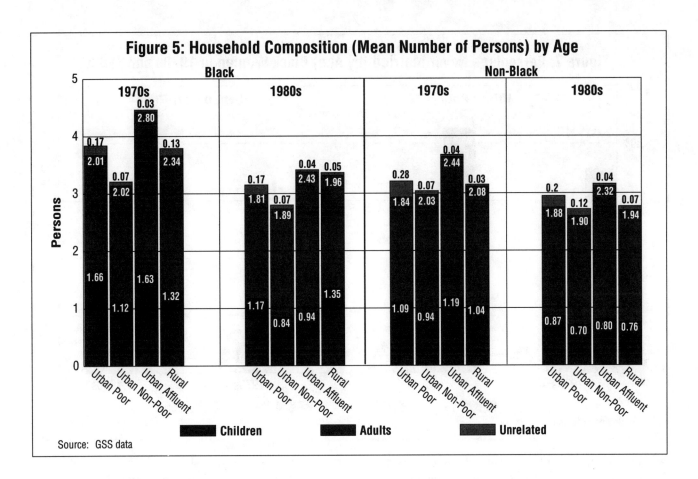

Figure 5: Household Composition (Mean Number of Persons) by Age

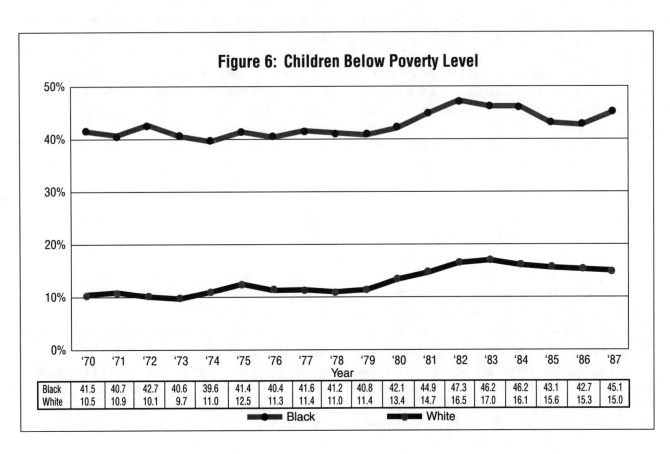

Figure 6: Children Below Poverty Level

	'70	'71	'72	'73	'74	'75	'76	'77	'78	'79	'80	'81	'82	'83	'84	'85	'86	'87
Black	41.5	40.7	42.7	40.6	39.6	41.4	40.4	41.6	41.2	40.8	42.1	44.9	47.3	46.2	46.2	43.1	42.7	45.1
White	10.5	10.9	10.1	9.7	11.0	12.5	11.3	11.4	11.0	11.4	13.4	14.7	16.5	17.0	16.1	15.6	15.3	15.0

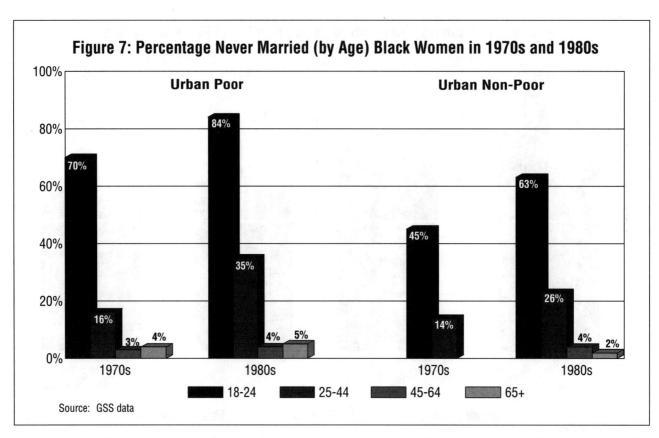

Figure 7: Percentage Never Married (by Age) Black Women in 1970s and 1980s

Source: GSS data

salient among African American women. Among Black women aged 30 to 34, the percentage who never married increased from 10 percent in 1960 to 35 percent in 1990. Among their White counterparts, the increase was from 6 to 12 percent. A few decades ago, late marriage and non-marriage were more prevalent among highly educated women. Recently, however, the least educated and often the economically disadvantaged are the least likely to enter marriage. Figure 7 shows the percentage of women who never married by age and economic status for Blacks in the 1970s and the 1980s. Among women aged 18 to 24, the percent never married grew from 70 to 84 for the Black urban poor and from 54 to 64 for the non-Black urban poor. Among their non-poor counterparts, the increase was from 45 to 63 percent for Blacks and from 42 to 59 percent for non-Blacks. Among women aged 25 to 44, the percentage never married rose from 16 percent to 35 percent for the Black urban poor. For their non-Black counterparts, the increase was much smaller, from 10 to 16 percent. Among the Black non-poor, aged 25 to 44, 14 percent never married in the 1970s compared with 26 percent in the 1980s. For non-Blacks, the percentages were 9 and 14, respectively.

Associated with this trend toward late marriage and non-marriage, at least up to 1980, there has been an increased acceptance of childbearing out-of-wedlock among both non-Black and Black Americans. Figure 8 shows the percent of never–married women aged 18 to 34 with one or more children for both Blacks and Whites by education. For Blacks with less than a high school education, the percentage of never–married women, 18 to 34, with at least one child grew from around 10 percent in 1960 to 40 percent in 1980. Among their White counterparts, that percentage grew from 2 percent or less to around 10 percent. This trend of childbearing without marriage, however, appeared to abate during the 1980s. Figure 9 shows the average number of children ever born by age of women in the 1970s and the 1980s. The decline was pervasive among non-Blacks but much less among poor Black Americans.

The relatively high prevalence of late marriage and non-marriage among poor African American women accounts for much but not all of the high likelihood of their being a head of household. Among those who have ever married, urban poor African American women are at the highest risk of

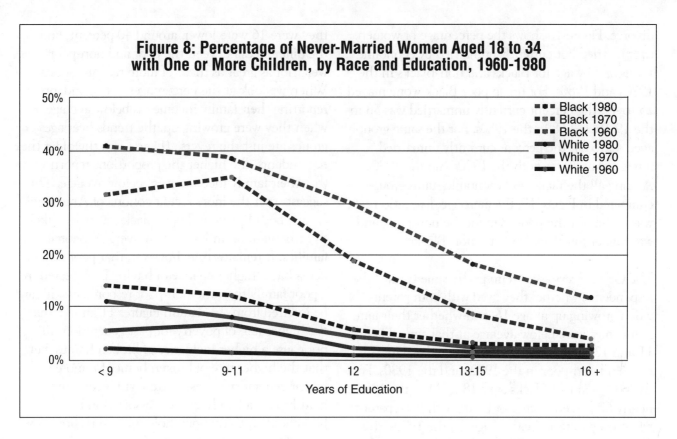

Figure 8: Percentage of Never-Married Women Aged 18 to 34 with One or More Children, by Race and Education, 1960-1980

Legend:
- Black 1980
- Black 1970
- Black 1960
- White 1980
- White 1970
- White 1960

X-axis: Years of Education (< 9, 9-11, 12, 13-15, 16 +)

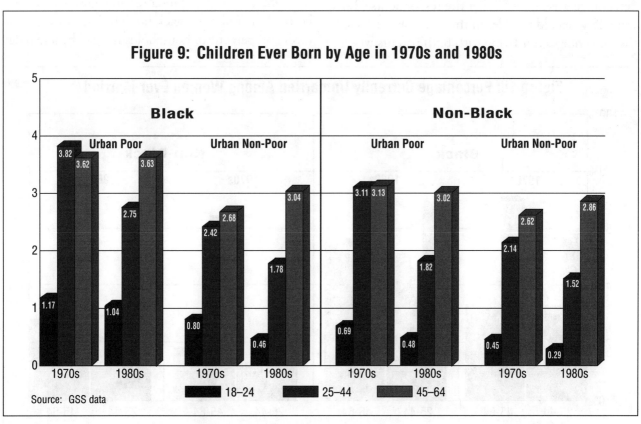

Figure 9: Children Ever Born by Age in 1970s and 1980s

Black

	Urban Poor	Urban Non-Poor
1970s	1.17 / 3.82 / 3.62	0.80 / 2.42 / 2.68
1980s	1.04 / 2.75 / 3.63	0.46 / 1.78 / 3.04

Non-Black

	Urban Poor	Urban Non-Poor
1970s	0.69 / 3.11 / 3.13	0.45 / 2.14 / 2.62
1980s	0.48 / 1.82 / 3.02	0.29 / 1.52 / 2.86

Legend: 18–24, 25–44, 45–64

Source: GSS data

divorce. Figure 10 shows the percentage of women ever married but currently unmarried by economic status and by age for Blacks and non-Blacks in the 1970s and 1980s. For urban poor Black women aged 25 to 44, the percent currently unmarried was 58 in the 1970s and 68 in the 1980s. For the same group aged 45 to 64, the percent currently unmarried remained at 70 for both the 1970s and the 1980s. Among all the racial and economic status groups compared in Figure 10, the marriage dissolution rate was higher for the poor than for the non-poor, and was higher for Blacks than for non-Blacks.

The GSS surveys asked retrospective questions of the respondents: whether they lived with both parents when growing up at age 16, and whether their family incomes were below average at that time. Figures 11 and 12 show the results by race and age for the poor and non-poor in the 1970s and the 1980s. For the poor younger Blacks aged 18 to 24 in the 1980s, nearly 60 percent were not living with both parents when they were 16 years of age. In the 1970s, this percentage was about 50. For the respondents who were 25 years old or older in the 1970s and 1980s, the percentages not living with both parents when

they were 16 were lower, around 40 percent, and the differences between the poor and non-poor were not as great as those of more recent cohorts. When we look at the percentages of respondents reporting their family incomes as below average when they were growing up, the trends over age groups are just the reverse (Figure 12): the older the respondents, the higher the proportions reporting that their family incomes were below average. This suggests that the more recent cohorts of Americans, among both Blacks and non-Blacks, were less likely to be brought up in lower-than-average-income families. It remains true, however, that poor respondents had a higher chance of having been reared in a poor family than the non-poor respondents. It can be inferred from the data in Figures 11 and 12 that the higher rate of poverty for past generations did not cause a higher incidence of broken homes, but that the higher rate of broken homes for more recent generations is associated with economic hardship for a family. A clear association between household type and household income is shown by the 1980 census data presented in Figure 13. For both Black and non-Black households, income level and percent of households headed by a female

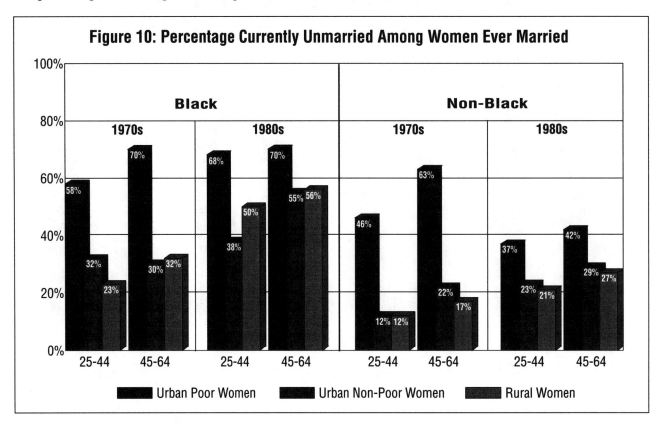

Figure 10: Percentage Currently Unmarried Among Women Ever Married

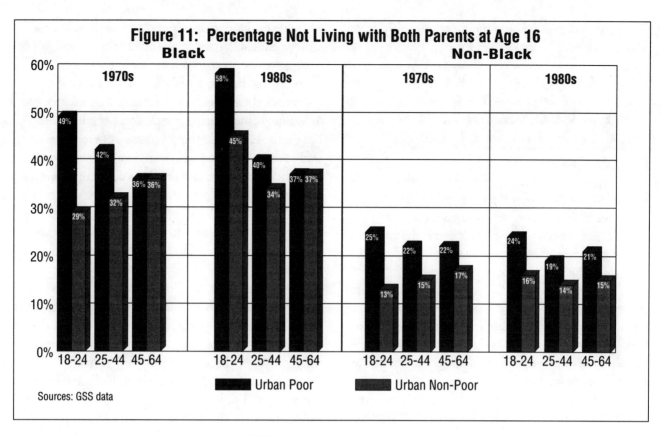

Figure 11: Percentage Not Living with Both Parents at Age 16

Sources: GSS data

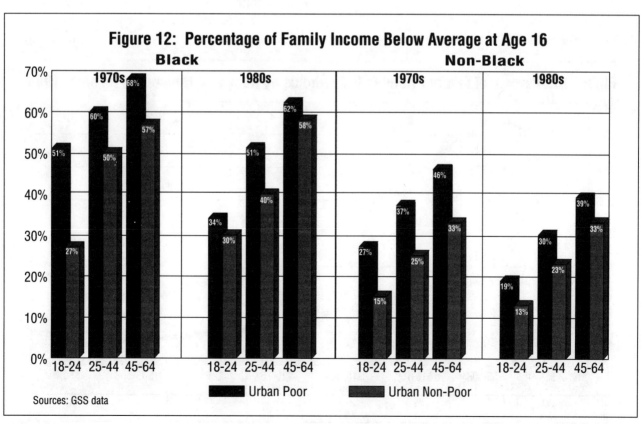

Figure 12: Percentage of Family Income Below Average at Age 16

Sources: GSS data

are negatively related, and such a relationship is much sharper for Blacks than for non-Blacks.

HUMAN CAPITAL: EDUCATION, EMPLOYMENT, AND WELL BEING

Educational attainment for Black Americans has been improving steadily over recent decades. However, the closing of the racial gap in education is much more pronounced in the increasing rate of high school completion by Black youth than in the completion rate of a college education. As shown in Figure 14, the high school completion rate for African Americans aged 20 to 24 rose from about 60 percent in 1968 to nearly 80 percent in 1988, compared with about 85 percent for their White counterparts in that same year. On the other hand, over the same period of 20 years, the college completion rate for African Americans aged 25 to 29 rose from 5 percent to about 10 percent while that of their White counterparts increased from 15 to nearly 25 percent.

Occupational achievement is strongly associated with educational attainment in American society.

More recently, African Americans with at least a college education are approaching the same level of occupational opportunities as that of their White counterparts. In fact, for Black women with a higher education, their career advancement may exceed that of White women with the same level of education. For example, in 1980 the percentage of employed workers aged 25 to 64 who were in executive, administrative, managerial, and professional occupations was 62 percent for White women with four years of college but 67 percent for Black women; and it was 83 percent for White women with a postgraduate education, compared with 86 percent for Black women.[7]

The recent trend toward increasing racial equality in occupational achievement for the better educated is by no means reflected in the situation at the other end of the spectrum. The contrasting rates of unemployment between Black and White Americans among the less advantaged are reason for concern. In fact, for Blacks under the age of 25, especially men, the disparity in labor force participation compared with their White counterparts became even greater during the economic recession of the 1980s.[8] Figure 15 depicts differential unem-

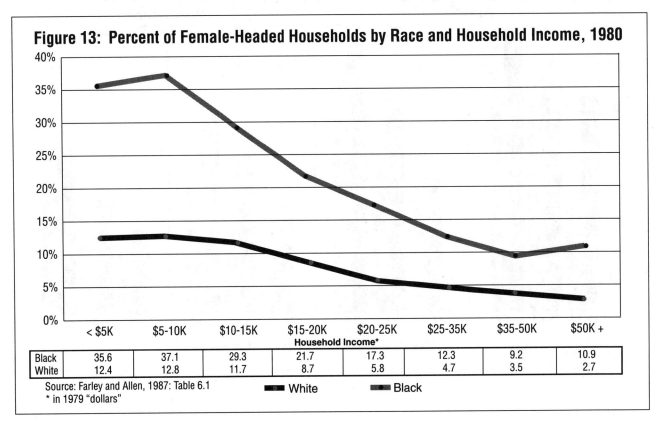

Figure 13: Percent of Female-Headed Households by Race and Household Income, 1980

	< $5K	$5-10K	$10-15K	$15-20K	$20-25K	$25-35K	$35-50K	$50K +
Black	35.6	37.1	29.3	21.7	17.3	12.3	9.2	10.9
White	12.4	12.8	11.7	8.7	5.8	4.7	3.5	2.7

Household Income*

Source: Farley and Allen, 1987: Table 6.1
* in 1979 "dollars"

━━ White   ━━ Black

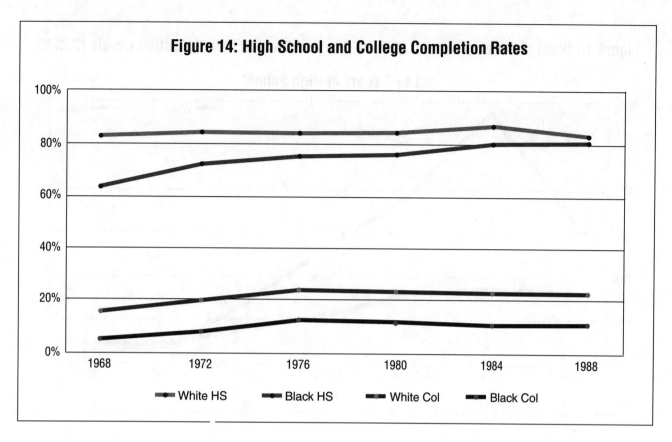

Figure 14: High School and College Completion Rates

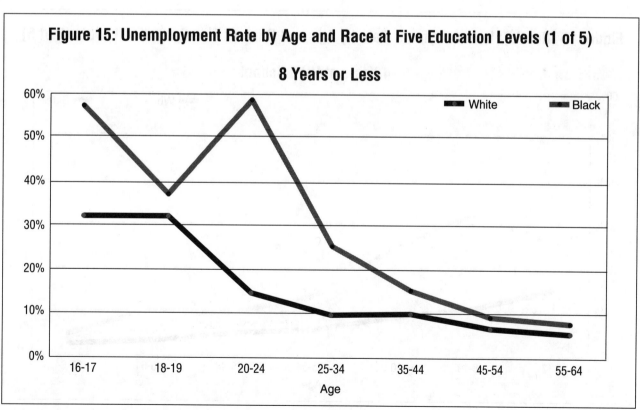

Figure 15: Unemployment Rate by Age and Race at Five Education Levels (1 of 5)

8 Years or Less

Figure 15 (Cont'd): Unemployment Rate by Age and Race at Five Education Levels (2 of 5)

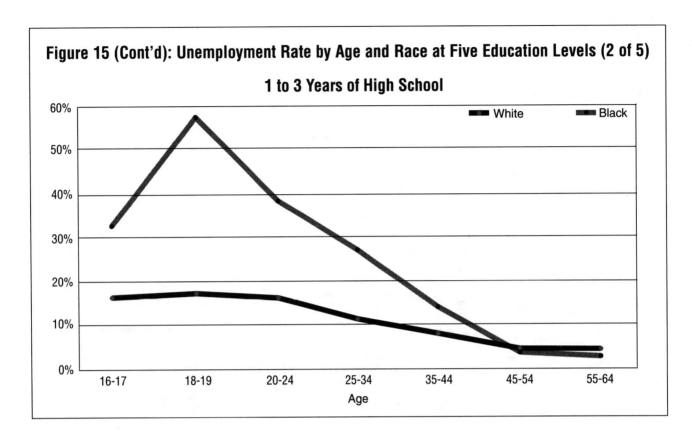

1 to 3 Years of High School

Figure 15 (Cont'd): Unemployment Rate by Age and Race at Five Education Levels (3 of 5)

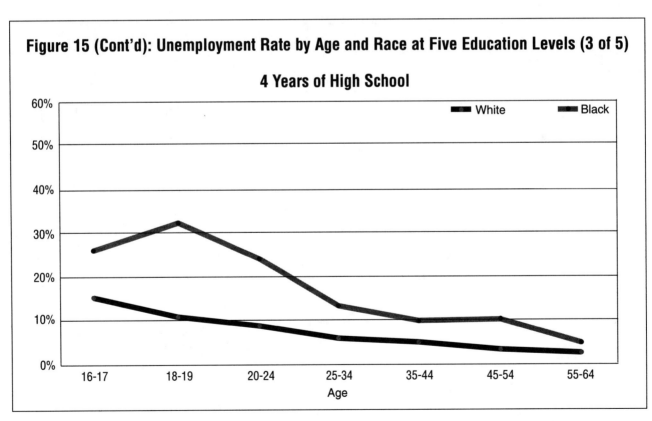

4 Years of High School

Figure 15 (Cont'd): Unemployment Rate by Age and Race at Five Education Levels (4 of 5)

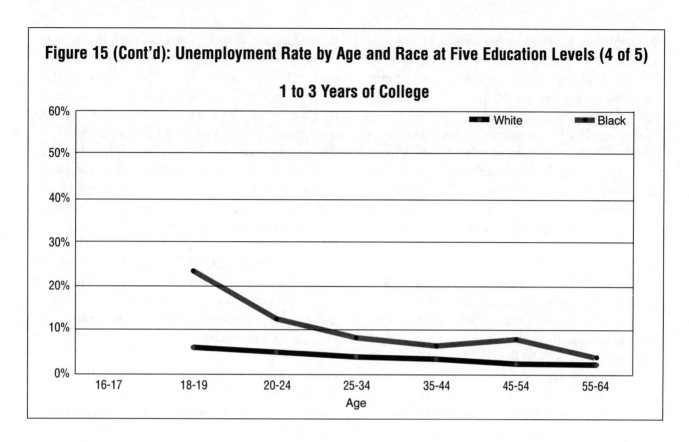

1 to 3 Years of College

Figure 15 (Cont'd): Unemployment Rate by Age and Race at Five Education Levels (5 of 5)

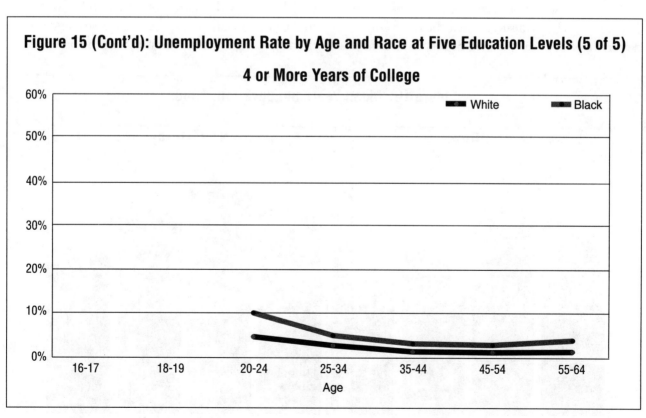

4 or More Years of College

ployment rates for 1988 by age for Blacks and Whites, controlling for level of education. It is clear that the racial disparity in the unemployment rate is greatest among age groups under 25 and among those who have not completed high school. For these young Blacks, the unemployment rate can be as high as 50 percent or more, whereas for Whites the highest unemployment rate hardly ever exceeds 30 percent. On the other hand, at the higher level of education with four years of college or more, little disparity exists, both Blacks and Whites enjoying a relatively low rate of unemployment.

Because level of education and percent of labor force participation differ by age, the Black and White urban poor and non-poor were again compared on these dimensions for both men and women using the GSS data for the 1980s (Figures 16 and 17). By the 1980s, racial differences in education were no longer as pronounced for the younger age cohorts under 45 years of age compared with those 45 or older, and the levels of educational attainment between the poor and non-poor were not as great as one would expect (Figure 16). The data suggest that the more crucial determinant of poverty should be sought elsewhere

than education. Figure 17 gives the different rates of having a "full-time occupation," defined as full-time work or full-time school during the week before the survey, by age and sex, for the urban poor and non-poor during the 1980s. The pattern is clear. The poor were less likely to be occupied full-time than were the non-poor; and Blacks were less likely to be occupied full-time than were non-Blacks at all comparable age and sex groups. In other words, young Black men with less than a high school education are at the highest risk of unemployment. However, the urban poor are not limited to Black men with less educational attainment. All urban poor of different ages and sexes are less likely to have a full-time occupation than their non-poor counterparts. Education may be one reason among others for different levels of occupational participation.

Health status is another aspect of the quality of life. Available in the GSS data is self-reported health information, i.e., whether one feels in excellent or good health. The comparative percentage reporting excellent or good health is presented in Figure 18 for the urban poor and non-poor by race, sex, and age in the 1980s. Again, it can be seen that the poor are

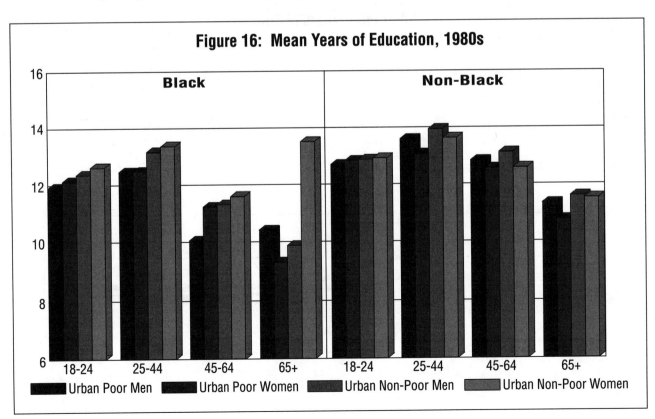

Figure 16: Mean Years of Education, 1980s

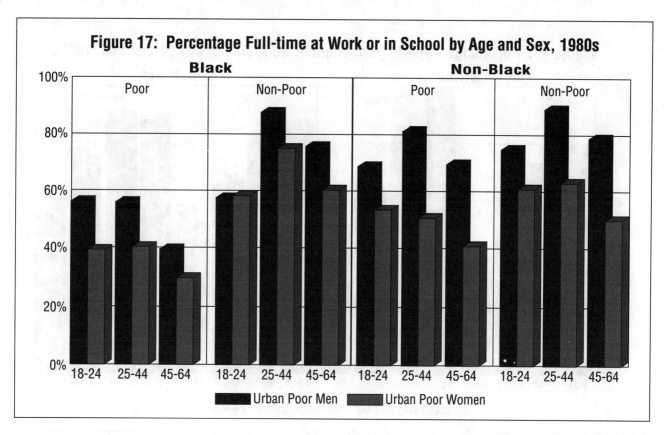

Figure 17: Percentage Full-time at Work or in School by Age and Sex, 1980s

less advantaged than the non-poor; and Blacks are worse off than non-Blacks for comparable sex and age groups.

A few indices of subjective well-being are also available in the GSS data: happiness with life in general, judgment on whether people are helpful most of the time, and fear of walking alone at night in one's own neighborhood. The survey questions originally read as follows:

Q. 154. Taken all together, how would you say things are these days—would you say that you are very happy, pretty happy, or not too happy?

Q. 158. Would you say that most of the time people try to be helpful, or that they are mostly just looking out for themselves?

Q. 234. Is there any area right around here—that is, within a mile—where you would be afraid to walk alone at night?

The responses to these questions are presented in Table 5 for the urban poor, urban non-poor, and residents of rural areas. It appears that differences in the level of happiness with life in general and in the feeling that other people are helpful most of the time are greater between races—the non-Blacks having a brighter outlook than Blacks—than between the poor and non-poor or between urban and rural residents. Perhaps because of the relatively higher concentration of the poor and of Blacks in more threatening or less safe environments, the Black urban poor were the most likely to fear walking alone at night in their own neighborhood.

POLITICAL PARTICIPATION AND INTER-RACIAL SENTIMENT

Prior to the passage of the Voting Rights Act of 1965, Blacks, especially those in southern states, had been discouraged from voting in political elec-

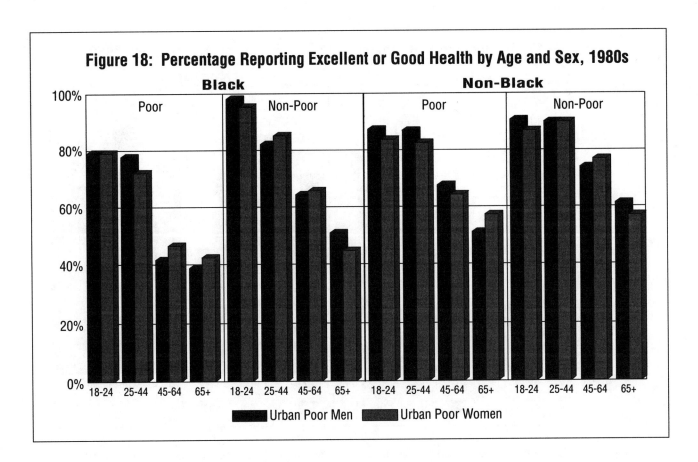

Figure 18: Percentage Reporting Excellent or Good Health by Age and Sex, 1980s

Table 5: Response to Questions About Happiness, Helpfulness, and Fear by Race, Economic Status, and Residence

Economic Status:	Black			Non-Black		
	Urban Poor	Urban Non-Poor	Rural	Urban Poor	Urban Non-Poor	Rural
PERCENTAGE VERY/PRETTY HAPPY WITH LIFE IN GENERAL						
	74.4	80.5	79.1	85.2	90.4	90.3
(N)	(1375)	(1694)	(293)	(4346)	(13331)	(3814)
PERCENTAGE FEELING THAT PEOPLE ARE HELPFUL MOST OF THE TIME						
	31.7	29.9	25.8	47.3	55.8	56.1
(N)	(934)	(1152)	(190)	(3045)	(9497)	(2610)
PERCENTAGE AFRAID TO WALK ALONE AT NIGHT						
	61.9	53.5	37.3	46.4	42.4	26.3
(N)	(934)	(1200)	(209)	(2789)	(8570)	(2462)

Source: GSS, 1972-1990.

tions. Only 5 percent of voting-age Blacks in Mississippi and 13 percent in Alabama, for example, were registered to vote as late as 1962.[9] The rapid increase since then in the participation of Blacks in political elections has been impressive. More than 60 percent of voting-age Blacks have registered to vote in presidential elections since 1968, and more than 50 percent actually voted. In congressional elections since 1974, 55 to 65 percent of voting-age Blacks have registered, and 34 to 43 percent actually voted (Figure 19). Black voter turnout still lagged behind that of Whites, however. The closing of this differential in political participation may not be imminent since in fact the Black population is younger, less educated, and less likely to own a home, all of which contribute to lower turnout.[10]

Black voters tend to vote for Black candidates for public office. The increase in the number of public offices held by elected Black politicians in recent decades has been significant. "In 1977 there were 4,311 Blacks holding elective offices, 0.9 percent of all elected officials in the country in that year. By 1987 there were 6,681 Black elected officials, representing 1.3 percent of all elected officials."[11] Nonetheless, Black representation in elected offices is still far from their 12 percent representation in the American population.

A number of experiential and attitudinal questions were asked specifically of the Black respondents in the GSS surveys for specific years, which may be relevant to the contemporary African American view of interracial relationships. Less than a quarter of Black respondents reported going to a high school where students were mostly White. Only 5 to 6 percent of Black respondents would choose to live in a neighborhood where the residents were mostly White. Only 6 to 7 percent of Black respondents considered most Whites to be trustworthy. And, as few as 13 percent of the respondents

Table 6: Response to Interracial Questions by Black Respondents

ATTENDED HIGH SCHOOL WHERE STUDENTS WERE

All Black	Mostly Black	Mostly White	No High School	Total	(N)
46.9%	23.9%	22.6%	6.7%	100.0%	(461)

PREFERRED A NEIGHBORHOOD WHERE RESIDENTS WERE

All Black	Mostly Black	Half-Half	Mostly White	Total	(N)
13.5%	17.9%	62.9%	5.6%	100.0%	(429)

TRUSTED WHITES:

Most Whites	Some Whites	No Whites	Total	(N)
6.9%	81.5%	11.6%	100.0%	(464)

COMPARED BLACK OCCUPATIONAL OPPORTUNITIES TO WHITES':

Almost Always the Same	Sometimes the Same	Almost Never the Same	Total	(N)
13.2%	54.6%	32.2%	100.0%	(463)

COMPARED BLACK OCCUPATIONAL OPPORTUNITIES NOW TO THE PAST:

Improved	The Same	Worse	Total	(N)
48.7%	31.8%	19.5%	100.0%	(462)

PREFERRED RACIAL NAME:

Black	Negro	Colored	Afro-American	No Difference	Total	(N)
51.2%	5.8%	4.9%	5.8%	32.3%	100.0%	(467)

Source: GSS, 1972-1990.

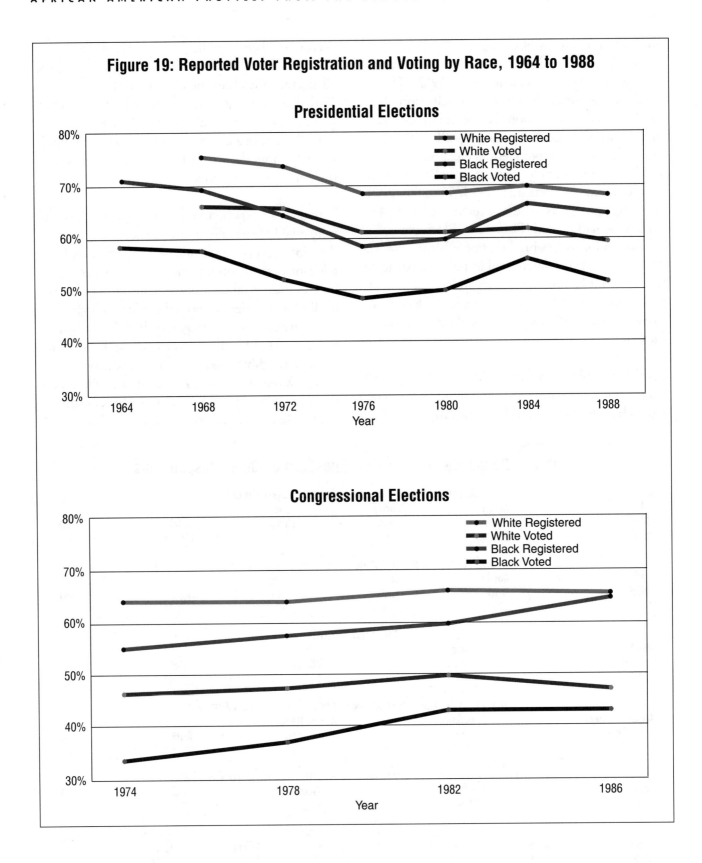

Figure 19: Reported Voter Registration and Voting by Race, 1964 to 1988

Presidential Elections

White Registered
White Voted
Black Registered
Black Voted

Congressional Elections

White Registered
White Voted
Black Registered
Black Voted

Table 7: Religious Affiliation by Race

Denomination	Black		Non-Black		
	Number	%	Number	%	Total
Catholic	270	7.8	6252	30.3	6522
Baptist	2050	59.2	3531	17.1	5581
Methodist Mainline	403	11.6	2530	12.3	2933
Protestant[a]	146	4.2	4638	22.5	4784
Fundamentalist Sects	412	11.9	2004	9.7	2416
No Religion	182	5.3	1673	8.1	1855
TOTAL	3463	100.0	20628	100.0	24091

Note: From cumulated GSS social surveys, 1972-1990.
[a]Episcopalians, Lutherans, Presbyterians.

thought that occupational opportunities were almost the same for Blacks as for Whites. However, nearly half of the respondents considered occupational opportunities for Blacks to have improved relative to the past (see Table 6).

RELIGION AND RACE

More than 90 percent of Americans identify with a religious denomination. Blacks are no exception. In fact, 95 percent identify with one religious group or other. Approximately 59 percent are Baptists, 8 percent Catholic, 4 percent mainline Protestant (Episcopalian, Lutheran, and Presbyterian), 12 percent Methodist, and 12 percent belong to various Protestant fundamentalist sects. This distribution differs considerably from that of the non-Black population, with 17 percent reporting their affiliation as Baptist, 30 percent as Catholic, 22 percent as mainline Protestant, 12 percent as Methodist, 10 percent as belonging to one or other Protestant sect, and 8 percent reporting no religion (see Table 7). These data are taken from the cumulated GSS surveys for 1972 to 1990. Other denominations were not included because of the very small sample sizes for Blacks. Little change occurred in these distributions from the 1970s to the 1980s.

Of greater interest is the change that occurred between the respondent's present religious affilia-

tion and affiliation at age 16. Eighty percent of Black Catholics at age 16 remained Catholic at the time of the surveys. Seven percent converted to the Baptist religion, 3 percent to various Protestant sects, and 8 percent reported no religious affiliation. However, movement occurred within Catholicism as well. At the time of the surveys, 80 percent of the Catholics were born Catholics, 15 percent were converts from Baptist Churches, and 5 percent from Methodist and mainline Protestant denominations. Less movement from and to Catholicism was reported by non-Blacks, 15 percent of adherents at age 16 leaving their religion and 10 percent of Catholic adults at the time of the surveys reporting that they were converts.

Movement occurred from and to other denominations also. The Baptist churches lost 18 percent of their Black adherents at age 16, mainly to the fundamentalist sects, but the greater losses were suffered by the mainline Protestant and the Methodist Churches, 37 and 33 percent, respectively. There was movement in the other direction as well. While only 7 percent of Black Baptists at the time of the survey reported that they were converts, as many as 36 percent of Black mainline Protestants and almost 20 percent of Methodists did so, most coming from Baptist churches. Among the non-

Black population, the pattern differs somewhat. The Methodists suffered the greatest loss, 39 percent, mostly to the mainline Protestant and the Baptist Churches. On the other hand, about 29 percent of current members reported conversions from mainline Protestant and Baptist Curches. Among White Baptists, 21 percent reported they were converts from various other denominations.

Among Blacks the fundamentalist sects lost the fewest members, 13 percent, with most of these joining Baptist congregations. Moreover, as many as 56 percent of current sectarians at the time of the surveys reported they had converted from other religions, the majority, 41 percent, coming from the Baptists. Among non-Blacks, the percentages are similar, 16 percent of members at age 16 leaving and 40 percent of current members having come from other religions, but only 14 percent coming from the Baptists.

Thirty percent of Black respondents who reported that they belonged to no religion at age 16 joined various fundamentalist sects or affiliated with the Baptist or Methodist churches. On the other hand, 83 percent of Blacks who at the time of the survey reported that they belonged to no religion had been affiliated with a Church at age 16, most, namely 55 percent, having been Baptist. Among non-Blacks,

55 percent with no religion at age 16 converted to some religion, while approximately 80 percent who identified themselves as having no religion at the time of the survey were once members of a religious group, most of them having been Catholic or mainline Protestants, 30 and 27 percent, respectively.

In spite of the movement back and forth between denominations, there was considerable stability between the overall percentages affiliated with each denomination at age 16 and at the time of the survey. Among Blacks the major exceptions are found among the Baptists, the fundamentalist sects, and those with no religion. Of the total cumulated sample of 3,175, only 6 percent were affiliated with Protestant sects at age 16 compared with 12 percent as adults; and only 1 percent professed no religion compared with 5 percent as adults. In the other direction, 67 percent identified themselves as Baptists at age 16 and only 60 percent as adults. Among non-Blacks the stability is more pronounced. Of 18,938 respondents, 7 percent belonged to Protestant sects at age 16 compared with 10 percent as adults, and 4 percent admitted to no religious affiliation at age 16 compared with 10 percent as adults. Differences among the marginals for the other denominations are no greater than 2.2 percent.

Table 8: Percentage of Church Attendance by Denomination and Race

| Denomination | Blacks | | | Total | | Non-Blacks | | | Total | |
	Rarely	Sometimes	Regularly	%	(N)	Rarely	Sometimes	Regularly	%	(N)
Catholics	27.5	40.5	32.0	100.0	269	26.2	27.2	46.6	100.0	6242
Baptists	20.2	45.1	34.7	100.0	2044	32.6	29.6	37.8	100.0	3516
Methodists	17.0	43.9	39.1	100.0	399	37.5	34.0	28.4	100.0	2520
Mainline Protestants	24.6	43.2	32.2	100.0	146	33.3	35.6	31.2	100.0	4618
Fundamentalist Sects	12.9	24.0	63.1	100.0	412	22.6	19.1	58.3	100.0	1999
No Religion	83.4	14.4	2.2	100.0	181	91.0	7.1	1.8	100.0	1652
Total					3451					20547

Note: Rarely = never, once a year, once or twice a year; Sometimes = several times a year, once a month, two or three times a month; Regularly = nearly every week, every week, several times a week.

More than 90 percent of Blacks and non-Blacks identify with a religious denomination but only approximately 36 percent within each group attend religious services "nearly every week" or more often (see Table 8). Attendance varies, however, between denominations. Among Catholics, 32 percent of Blacks and 47 percent of non-Blacks attend nearly every week or more. Among the fundamentalist sectarians, these percentages jump to 63 and 58 percent, respectively, and among the other Protestant denominations that percentage is 33 for both Blacks and non-Blacks.

Whereas 50 percent of all Blacks are classified as urban non-poor in this study, as many as 64 percent of Black Catholics belong to that category (see Table 9). This contrast is not as pronounced among non-Blacks. While 62 percent are classified as urban non-poor, 69 percent of the Catholics fall into the category. Furthermore, of the total GSS cumulative sample, 14 percent of the respondents identified themselves as African American or Black but only 4 percent of the Catholics so identified. The data suggest some overrepresentation of urban non-poor among Catholics, especially among Blacks, and certainly a significant underrepresentation of urban poor and rural (mostly poor) Blacks. To what extent is the failure to evangelize this segment of the Black population due to lack of effort or to the problem of cultural differences reflecting, in part, socioeconomic status?

Such differences may be crucial also to explain the relative lack of success in recruiting young Black men for the Catholic priesthood. Approximately 4 percent of Catholics are Black but only 1.6 percent of Catholic seminarians in a recent survey identified themselves as Black.[12]

Blacks are overrepresented in some dioceses compared to others. Table 10 lists dioceses by the percent of Blacks in the total population of the territory they cover. Some, such as Jackson, Miss., and Washington, D.C., approach 40 percent. Others, such as Scranton and Green Bay, have less than 1 percent. Nonetheless, all have a mission toward this group if the Church is to be more successful in its evangelization program. To paraphrase John Coleman, it is imperative that Catholicism in America expand its store of heroes and heroines to include Blacks if it wishes to communicate with Blacks. And this is a task for all Catholics.

A FINAL NOTE

We have used the terms "Black" and "African American" interchangeably in this report. It may be interesting to add this note. Less than 6 percent of Black respondents would prefer to be called "negro"; less than 6 percent would like to be

Table 9: Percent Distribution of Residence and Poverty Level by Denomination and Race

Denomination	Blacks					Non-Blacks				
	Urban Poor	Non-Poor	Rural	Total %	(N)	Urban Poor	Non-Poor	Rural	Total %	(N)
Catholic	32.6	63.6	3.8	100.0	258	20.8	68.6	10.6	100.0	5934
Baptist	42.9	47.0	10.1	100.0	1927	20.2	53.1	26.7	100.0	3372
Methodist	38.5	51.0	10.4	100.0	384	15.9	57.3	26.8	100.0	2435
Mainline Protestant	32.9	59.3	7.8	100.0	140	17.1	63.7	19.2	100.0	4462
Fundamentalist Sect	43.5	47.1	9.4	100.0	393	24.6	54.4	21.0	100.0	1924
No Religion	35.8	61.3	2.9	100.0	173	22.1	66.2	11.7	100.0	1587
Total					3275					19714

Table 10: Percentage of Blacks in Total Population by Diocese

20% and Above	10 to 19%	5 to 9%	3 to 5%	0 to 2%
Alexandria	Austin	Arlington	Amarillo	Albany
Shreveport	Beaumont	Bridgeport	Anchorage	Allentown
Atlanta	Belleville	Buffalo	Boston	Altoona - Johnstown
Baltimore	Camden	Columbus	Covington	Baker
Baton Rouge	Charlotte	Fort Wayne - South Bend	Denver	Bismarck
Biloxi	Cincinnati	Fort Worth	El Paso	Boise
Birmingham	Cleveland	Grand Rapids	Fairbanks	Brownsville
Brooklyn	Dallas	Hartford	Fresno	Burlington
Charleston	Galveston - Houston	Indianapolis	Harrisburg	Cheyenne
Chicago	Gary	Kalamazoo	Jefferson City	Corpus Christi
Detroit	Houma - Thibodaux	Kansas City	Joliet	Crookston
Jackson	Kansas City - St. Joseph	Lansing	Monterey	Davenport
Lafayette, LA	Little Rock	Milwaukee	Peoria	Des Moines
Memphis	Los Angeles	Nashville	Rockford	Dodge City
Mobile	Louisville	Oklahoma City	Sacramento	Dubuque
New Orleans	Miami	Omaha	Salinas	Duluth
Philadelphia	New York	Owensboro	San Angelo	Erie
Raleigh	Newark	Paterson	Seattle	Evansville
Richmond	Oakland	Pittsburgh	Springfield, IL	Fall River
Savannah	Orlando	Reno - Las Vegas	Springfield, MA	Fargo
St. Augustine	Pensacola - Talahassee	Rochester	Stockton	Gallup
Washington	St. Louis	Rockville Center	Syracuse	Gaylord
	Wilmington	Saginaw	Tucson	Grand Island
		San Antonio	Wheeling - Charleston	Green Bay
		San Bernardino	Wichita	Greensburg
		San Diego		Helena
		San Francisco		Honolulu
		St. Petersburg		Juneau
		Toledo		La Croix
		Trenton		Lafayette, IN
		Tulsa		Lincoln
		Youngstown		Madison
				Manchester
				Marquette
				New Ulm
				Norwich
				Ogdensburg
				Orange
				Phoenix
				Portland, ME
				Portland, OR
				Providence
				Pueblo
				Rapid City
				Salt Lake City
				Santa Fe
				Santa Rosa
				Scranton
				Sioux City
				Sioux Falls
				Spokane
				Springfield, CA
				St. Cloud
				St. Paul - Minneapolis
				Steubenville
				Surfview
				Winona
				Worcester
				Yakima

referred to as "Afro-American"; half preferred to be called "Black"; and one-third indicated no preference (Table 6).

SUMMARY

African Americans constituted 12 percent of the total U.S. population in 1991. Within-group differences among Blacks increased during the decades of the 1970s and 1980s. The data presented in this study are mainly from the General Social Surveys cumulated over the decades of the 1970s and 1980s. Profiles of the Black urban poor, the urban non-poor, the affluent, and the rural Blacks are presented.

African Americans are three to four times more likely than Whites to be poor. And they are less likely to be affluent, only 5 to 6 percent reporting incomes of $50,000 or higher. The level of Black children living in poverty exceeded 40 percent in the 1970s, and to some extent that level increased during the 1980s.

Since 1960, the trend toward marrying later or not at all has been characteristic of both Blacks and other Americans but was especially salient among Black women. Associated with this trend has been an increased acceptance of childbearing out-of-wedlock among both Blacks and non-Blacks. Among all the racial and economic status groups, the marriage dissolution rate was higher for the poor, Black and non-Black, than for the non-poor, and was higher for Blacks than for non-Blacks. For Black and non-Black households, income level and percent of households headed by a female are negatively related, and such a relationship is much sharper for Blacks than for non-Blacks.

Over the past years there has been a closing of the racial gap in education, but this trend is much more pronounced in the increasing rate of high school completion by Black youth than in the completion rate of a college education. Recently, African Americans with at least a college education are approaching the same level of occupational oppor-

tunities as that of their White counterparts. In fact, the career advancement of Black women with a higher education may exceed that of White women with the same level of education. Unfortunately, the contrasting rates of unemployment between Black and White Americans among the less advantaged are reason for concern. The racial disparity in the unemployment rate is greatest among younger age groups and among those who have not completed high school, reaching as high as 50 percent or more for Blacks under age 25 who have not completed high school. Education, however, is not the most crucial determinant of poverty. Urban poverty spawns more poverty.

Since passage of the Voting Rights Act of 1965, there has been a rapid increase in the participation of Blacks in political elections, and the increase in the number of public offices held by elected Black politicians in recent decades has been significant. Nonetheless, Black representation in elected offices is still far from their present representation in the American population.

More than 90 percent of Americans identify with a religious denomination. Blacks are no exception. Most are Baptists. Few are Catholic or members of the mainline Protestant Churches. Some "switching" of denominations takes place between the age of sixteen and adulthood. Generally, however, the denominations gain as much as they lose, with the exception of the fundamentalist sects who gain much more than they lose. Significant net gains are reported among those who report "no religion" as adults. In spite of high percentages of religious belonging, only 36 percent of Blacks and non-Blacks attend religious services "nearly every week" or more often. Most Black Catholics are classified as urban non-poor, suggesting the need for more aggressive evangelization programs among the urban poor and rural Blacks.

NOTES

1. "Black Americans" reported in the Census are most likely the native-born Americans of African ancestry. Foreign-born Blacks, by racial category, from countries in African and Caribbean regions were estimated to be about 1.4 million based on the 1980 census. According

to records from Immigration and Naturalization Services, about 1 million immigrants from these two regions were admitted to the United States during the 1980s. By 1990, therefore, the foreign-born Black population would be around 2.4 million, or nearly 1 percent of the total U.S. population.

2. William J. Wilson. *The Truly Disadvantaged: The Inner City, the Underclass, and Public Policy* (Chicago: University of Chicago Press, 1987).

3. John Reid. "Black America in the 1980s." *Population Bulletin* 37(4) (Washington, D.C.: The Population Reference Bureau, Inc., 1982).

4. William P. O'Hare, Kelvin M. Pollard, Taynia L. Mann, and Mary M. Kent. "African Americans in the 1990s." *Population Bulletin*, 46(1) (Washington, D.C.: The Population Reference Bureau, Inc., 1991).

5. James A. Davis and Tom W. Smith. *General Social Surveys, 1972-1990: Cumulative Codebook* (Chicago: National Opinion Research Center, 1990).

6. Reid, "Black America in the 1980s"; O'Hare, et al., "African Americans in the 1990s."

7. Renolds Farley and Walter R. Allen. *The Color and the Quality of Life in America* (New York: Russell Sage Foundation, 1987, p. 276).

8. Ibid., Figure 8.1.

9. O'Hare, et al., "African Americans in the 1990s," p. 33.

10. Ibid., p. 34.

11. Ibid.

12. E. Hemrick and D. R. Hoge. *Seminarians in Theology: A National Profile* (Washington, D.C.: United States Catholic Conference, 1985).

UNDERSTANDING AFRICAN AMERICAN FAMILY REALITIES

D R .   A N D R E W   B I L L I N G S L E Y

By tradition and by preference African Americans are family oriented. Family is the central and most highly valued reality in all of African American life. That is true historically. It is true today.

For many, accustomed to reading the scholarly literature, policy papers, or the daily press, these assertions about the primacy of family in African American life will seem odd.

Despite the pressures in society that have taken their toll on African American family stability, still today the overwhelming majority of African American people live in families. This is true, even by the very narrow definition of family that the U.S. Census Bureau uses. This definition requires persons living together in the same household and related to each other by marriage, blood, or adoption. Even by this definition, some 70 percent of all African American households are family households. And they live in a wide variety of family patterns. Moreover, the other 30 percent of African American households is primarily single-person households or individual Black

adults living alone in their own house, apartment, or room. Indeed, these single-person households are among the fastest growing sectors of the African American community. They are young persons who have never been married, individuals separated or divorced living alone, and widows and widowers living alone. Most of these, however, are never-married persons. The trends in this regard are shown in Table 1.

According to the U.S. Census, never-married Black men accounted for some 26.9 percent of all Black men over 15 in 1960. By 1980 this figure had escalated to 41.1 percent and by 1991 to 44.8 percent. A similar trend was shown for Black women. Further swelling the ranks of adult Black single persons have been the increase

FAMILY IS THE CENTRAL AND MOST HIGHLY VALUED REALITY IN ALL OF AFRICAN AMERICAN LIFE.

in divorce and the smaller numbers of widowed persons. Combining all these sources of singlehood in 1991 shows that nearly 57 percent of Black men over 15 and nearly 62 percent of Black women over 15 were not married. This represented an enormous increase over just 30 years ago in 1960 when just 34 percent of Black men and 40 percent of Black women were single. This means that many young persons are postponing marriage and others are avoiding it altogether. Increasing numbers of these decide to set up housekeeping in their own single-person household.

But in the African American experience, to say that persons live alone in their own house is not to say that they are devoid of meaningful family ties. Thus, in *Climbing Jacob's Ladder*,[1] we offer a definition of family that is much broader, more flexible than the Census Bureau definition. We do not require people to live in the same house to be family. And we do not require them to be related only by marriage, blood, or legal adoption.

In this view, family may best be defined as an intimate association of individuals, related to each other by a variety of means including all the above, but also by informal adoption, adaptation, and cohabitation. The essence of the family relationship is that a group of people have a sense of belonging together in keeping with their heritage, and that they assume responsibility to each other and for each other—an intimate association of mutual responsibility and caring. According to this definition, family is an even more widespread phenomenon in the African American community than the census figures indicate.

FAMILY HOUSEHOLDS

The place of the family in African American culture is further buttressed by the rising Black population. Growing substantially faster than the national average, the Black population reached more than 30 million by 1991. And most of these are family households. Thus, the actual numbers of Black households have expanded enormously even as the average size of each household has been on the decline. As shown by Table 2 the number of Black households increased from some 4.8 million in 1960 to almost 7.3 million in 1980 and to nearly 10.7 million by

Table 1: Marital Status of African Americans 15 Years of Age and Over*

	1960	1970	1980	1990	1991
NEVER MARRIED					
Men	26.9 %	35.6 %	41.1%	43.4 %	44.8 %
Women	21.7	22.7	33.7	36.9	38.7
MARRIED CURRENTLY					
Men	63.3	56.9	48.9	45.1	43.1
Women	60.3	54.0	44.6	40.2	38.7
DIVORCED					
Men	2.4	3.1	6.3	8.1	8.8
Women	3.7	4.4	8.7	11.2	11.0
WIDOWED					
Men	4.6	4.4	3.7	3.4	3.3
Women	14.3	13.8	13.0	11.6	11.9

*Sources: *Current Population Reports, Population Characteristics*, U.S. Bureau of the Census, p. 20, no. 464;
"The Black Population in the U.S. March 1991," U.S. Department of Commerce, 1992, 5.

Table 2: Number and Average Size of African American Households, 1960 to 1991

Year	Number (Millions)	Percent Change Over Previous Years	Average Size
1960	4.779	—	3.8
1970	6.180	29.3	3.5
1980	7.262	17.5	3.3
1990	10.486	41.1	2.9
1991	10.671	1.8	2.9

1991. Thus the actual numbers of Black households increased by more than 44 percent between 1980 and 1990 and have doubled since 1960.

MARRIED-COUPLE FAMILIES

What sometimes confuses readers of family studies is that the raw numbers of persons, households, and families are often not given, instead showing percentages only. These percentages often obscure the fact that the actual numbers of Black families have continued to expand over the years even as other living arrangements have expanded faster. Thus the actual number of Black families has expanded from 3.4 million in 1950 to 7.5 million by 1991 (U.S. Census).

These data support our contention that families are a primary element in African American life even today. Even married-couple families have continued to grow in numbers. Indeed the actual numbers of Black married-couple families increased from 3.5 million in 1983 to 3.7 million in 1988 and to 3.8 million by 1990. And these married-couple families continue to be the norm in African American communities.[2]

CHILDREN—THE MOST ESSENTIAL PART OF THE FAMILY SYSTEM

Once we recognize the centrality of family in African American life, we must immediately call attention to the fact that children are still the highest priority for the African American family.

African Americans care deeply about their children, and they want the best for them. Even very poor people, even people in desperate straits of despair, often want the best for their children. They put their children ahead of themselves. Some mothers care so much for their children that they will leave them in hospitals after birth, because they believe their children will get better care than if they take them into the nights of despair awaiting their mothers. And we call them border babies and say very bad things about these mothers. We should have learned better from Tony Morrison in "Beloved." She tried to teach us that during slavery, some mothers would rather see their children die and go to heaven than to see them return to slavery. Caring deeply for children is an African American cultural tradition.

But many would ask, is this tradition alive today? The answer is yes. Consider the following fact. There are some 10 million African American children alive today. Of these, 9 out of 10 are being cared for by their parents. Some one out of ten or nearly a million Black children are not being raised by their parents for a variety of reasons. What happens to these 1 million children? Only about two out of ten, some 200,000, are cared for by the entire child welfare system, federal, state, and local, public and private. Who cares for the other eight out of ten of these children? They are cared for primarily by their relatives, their extended families, and most especially by their grandmothers. It is a family affair. Surely no other people, no other ethnic group can lay such high claim to such demonstrated caring about the well being of their children.[3]

In *Climbing Jacob's Ladder,* we cite numerous examples of the care for children. These are not isolated examples of the extended family and community institutions reaching out to help care for the community's children. Indeed, Robert Hill has pointed out that 90 percent of all Black children born out of wedlock are still being raised in three-generational families, usually headed by their grandmothers. The extended family is alive and functional in the African American community today, taking major responsibility for the care of children.

But in addition to extended and augmented family members helping with the care of children, there is still another African American cultural tradition at work today: successful Black individuals in the community reaching out to help provide guidance to other people's children. We cite the work of Kent and Carmen Amos, an upper-middle-class Black couple in Washington who brought Black high school youth into their home every day after school for ten years. During this time more than fifty youth were provided mentoring, which enabled most of them to avoid the pitfalls awaiting Black youth today. There are thousands of examples of this. And since there are far more Black adults who are working, middle, and upper class than poor, the promise of this self-help tradition is quite enormous.

Thirdly, beyond extended family and other individuals, there is still another African American cultural legacy that often helps parents raise their children. That institution is the Black church.

In *Climbing Jacob's Ladder,* we cite numerous Black churches with exemplary community outreach programs. And in a recent survey of some 630 Black churches, we found that two thirds of them offer some type of outreach program. A common type of outreach program is one designed to help parents and schools care for and teach their children.

A good example of this is the Friendship Baptist Church in Columbus, Ga. After celebrating its one hundredth anniversary, the church decided to establish two new community outreach programs. The church surveyed the inner-city community determining that its most pressing need was for help in child care and child rearing. So the church, starting with its own funds and then raising more, established two programs for families in the community, not necessarily for members of the church. The programs are for working parents with modest incomes. One is a child development center operated by the church for infants whose parents must go to work. At modest cost, the children and parents get quality care and guidance from professionals. The second is an after-school program for children aged 6 to 13 whose parents work and who might otherwise be latch-key children. They will have a healthy, wholesome experience with adult supervision until their parents get home. The church also works with the parents in helping them and the schools provide guidance and support to these children.

It is consistent with the values of the African American community that neighbors, in this organized manner, reach out to help raise the children. This church knows that the children belong not only to their parents, but to the entire community.

There are more than 75,000 organized Black churches in the nation today, with more than 25 million members. They are

GENERALIZA-TIONS ABOUT AFRICAN AMERICAN FAMILY PATTERNS OFTEN DEGENERATE INTO STEREOTYPES BECAUSE THEY FAIL TO PUT FAMILIES INTO A HOLISTIC PERSPECTIVE.

the oldest, the strongest, the most independent, the best led, the richest, the most family oriented, the most affirming institutions in the whole African American community. Already they provide more jobs, more housing, more after-school programs, more volunteers, more positive self-esteem, more political clout, and more economic clout and garner more respect and support than any other institution in the community.

THE VITALITY OF AFRICAN AMERICAN FAMILY LIFE

Often we read about the problems of the Black family. Not often enough do we read about the strength, the potential, the power, the resourcefulness, the vitality of the Black family. It is important to add this dimension to our knowledge so that we get a "holistic" picture of the family and become more aware of the strengths, power, and potential of these families.

CHALLENGES FACING AFRICAN AMERICAN FAMILIES

Make no mistake; the challenges facing contemporary African American families are enormous. Indeed they are staggering. As I said in my book, *Climbing Jacob's Ladder,* "It is ironic, perhaps, that what three centuries of slavery and one century of near slavery could not destroy may be destroyed by a few years of progress."

What are some of these challenges?

In an interim report entitled *Opening Doors for American Children* (1990), the National Commission on Children under the leadership of Senator Jay Rockefeller IV cited some of these conditions.

The experience of growing up in the United States today is very different than it was just a generation ago. Sweeping social and economic changes since the 1960s have fundamentally altered the form of many American families, the way they live, and the world in which they raise their children. Changing patterns of marriage and family formation, the dramatic entry of women into the paid labor force, and the declining economic status of many families with children have been widely reported and analyzed.

... At every income level, in all racial and ethnic groups, and in every region of the country, these changes have challenged the routines, traditions, and family values of generations of Americans. ...

For the nation they raise important and often troubling questions about the health and well-being of this and future generations of children and the capability and commitment of their parents to care for and nurture them (7).

Indeed so. And if these are the challenges facing American children, imagine the force of these challenges as they confront African American families and children, who in addition to all the burdens borne by others, must still exist in the shadows of the nation, in the words of DuBois, "behind the veil."

More specifically, the National Commission set forth these major issues facing American children:

- The need for adequate parents or other caring adults

- The need to move out of poverty

- The need for resolution of the crisis in health care

- The need for school readiness

- The need for reorienting services for children with a focus on prevention and coordination

FAMILY STRUCTURAL DIVERSITY

When searching for the meaning of the recent transformation in the African American community, one must keep in mind that no single family form characterizes the Black community. Instead, a wide variety of structures have arisen. For the hundred-year period between the end of slavery and the aftermath of World War II, the structure of African American family life was characterized by a remarkable degree of stability. Specifically, the core of the traditional African American family system has been the nuclear family composed of husband and wife and their children. Divorce was rare, and couples stayed together until the death of a spouse. Children lived with their parents until maturity and then started their own families. Other elements in the traditional African American family system are the extended family, a carryover from the African heritage, and the augmented family with the inclusion of non-relatives. This, then, is the traditional African American family system. After World War II, however, the decline became phenomenal and this traditional African American family structure began to give way to a wide variety of alternative forms.

As late as 1960, when uneducated Black men could still hold good paying blue-collar jobs in the industrial sector, fully 78 percent of all Black families with children were headed by married couples. By 1970, only 64 percent of African American families with children were headed by married couples. This declined steadily to 54 percent by 1975; to 48 percent by 1980; and to a minority of 40 percent by 1985. The trend is likely to continue. Meanwhile, one of the alternatives to the traditional family, the single-parent family, particularly the female-headed family, has escalated enormously over the past generation. Consisting of a minority of 22 percent of families with children in 1960, this family form had increased to 33 percent by 1970, to 44 percent by 1975, to 49 percent by 1980, and to 57 percent by 1985.

What, then, has taken the place of the traditional family system? At least nine alternative family structures have arisen in post-industrial America to characterize the contemporary pattern of African American family diversity. Some of these alternatives are as follows:

1. *Single-Person Households*. Increasing numbers of African American adults are living in single-person households.

2. *Cohabitation*. Small but expanding numbers of adults are choosing to live with another person of the opposite sex and sometimes of the same

sex in a marriage-like relationship without benefit of legal marriage. While fewer than 5 percent of Black adults live in cohabitation relationships, the numbers are expanding rapidly.

3. *Children Without Marriage*. In 1983, there were 3,043,000 Black single-parent households (compared with 3,486,000 married-couple households and 2,386,000 non-family households). Of these, 1,989,000 were single parents with children under 18. Of these, 127,000 were male-headed families and 1,864,000 were female-headed. The 872,000 Black female-headed families with children 18 and over must surely be distinguished from the 1.8 million who have children under 18.

What is the source of their single-parent status? Among men 98,000 were never married, 79,000 were divorced, 68,000 were widowed, and 64,000 were married with absent spouses due to incarceration, long-term illness, or desertion. Among women the same pattern was seen. The largest group, comprising 899,000, was never married. Next were divorced mothers at 655,000; followed by those married with absent spouses, 646,000; and widows with children, 534,000.

By 1986, single-parent families from all sources had expanded. Overall, the number had increased to 3,242,000, representing 33 percent of the 9.8 million Black households.

4. *Married Couples Without Children*. This group, too, has been expanding among African American families.

5. *Married Couples with Children*. By 1986, despite population growth, there were only 1,997,000 Black married-couple families with children. This amounted to a declining 20 percent of the 9.8 million Black households.

6. *Children and Grandparents*. Altogether there were 548,000 Black extended families in 1983, accounting for 6 percent of the 8.9 million households. By 1986, this had expanded to 607,000 extended families, representing a similar proportion of the 9.8 million households.

SOCIAL CLASS DIVERSITY

If the African American people are characterized by diverse and rapidly changing patterns of family structure—rather than by any one family structure—this diversity is equally true with respect to social class. As important and troubling as is the celebrated "underclass," it represents only a small fraction of all African American families. There are a number of reasons why it is important to take a holistic view of the African American community. First, it helps to avoid stereotypes. A focus on only one stratum tends to suggest that it is characteristic of Black families. Second, a view of the entire class structure helps to show that there is upward and downward mobility. It shows, for example, that one class may be expanding at the expense of another or that one class may be the source of expansion in other classes. Additionally, a view of the entire class structure shows the dynamism in the African American community. It helps to avoid the often-repeated suggestion that the underclass is permanent, or that there are only two classes—underclass and middle class—or that there is no Black upper class, all of which are part of today's fashionable but false conventional wisdom. More importantly, a view of the entire class spectrum will reveal that it is none of the above classes but the Black blue-collar working class that is the backbone of the Black community. Finally, it will show that it is precisely this working class that is being decimated by changing technological, economic, and social conditions which, in turn, constitute the major reason for the demise of traditional African American family patterns. From the perspective of social change and reform, then, an appreciation of the entire social-class structure of the Black community is important.

The concept of social class suggests that some families have greater resources, higher status, and more options than others in managing their lives. The three most common indexes for measuring social class are the amount of family income, the educational level, or the occupational prestige of the family head. Each index has advantages and limitations. However, the family income measure is superior to the others as a measure of economic and social well-being.

FIVE SOCIAL CLASSES

In our own work, we have identified five distinct social class strata in the African American community. Based primarily on level of family income, complemented by education, occupation, and style of life, these five strata include (1) the underclass, consisting of poor families where no member has a permanent attachment to the work force; (2) the working poor, where despite working for low wages, they are not able to earn above the poverty line; (3) the non-poor working class, composed of unskilled and semi-skilled blue-collar workers with earnings above the poverty line; (4) the middle class, comprised primarily of white-collar skilled and professional workers with family income above the median for all families; and (5) a small Black upper class of families with high incomes and substantial wealth as well as social and economic influence.[4]

One of the most striking features of the entire social class structure is that while the underclass has been expanding over this period, the non-poor working class was declining by almost the exact same magnitude, from 44 percent in 1969 to 36 percent in 1983 and to 34 percent of all African American families by 1986. This shows with dramatic clarity that the underclass is expanding at the expense of the non-poor working class. In turn, this removes a considerable amount of the mystery as to why the underclass is growing and from where this growth is coming.

Still further support for the socialization of Black children with pioneering role models is provided by the small group of Black families who have moved to the top of the socioeconomic structure by the ownership and management of their own business enterprises. Each year *Black Enterprise* magazine profiles the Black families owning the largest 100 Black businesses. Few more inspiring role models of upper-class Blacks can be found than the John H. Johnson family of Chicago, the George A. Russell family of Atlanta, or the Earl Graves family of New York.

These families are not likely to be as well-known as some other upper-class families, such as the Jesse Jackson family, which made such a positive impression at the 1988 Democratic National Convention, or the Bill Cosby family, whose example, achievement, and philanthropy make us all proud. They are important role models, nevertheless, especially in a society which places such high values on private enterprise and in areas where Blacks need a great deal of encouragement. These families at the top of the socioeconomic structure are few in number, but the important point is that their ranks are increasing.

In 1969, there were some 143,000 families in this Black upper-class stratum comprising a tiny 3 percent of all African American families in the nation. Half of all these families had working wives; in the other half, the husbands worked while the wives were full-time homemakers. By 1983, this stratum had expanded to embrace some 267,000 families comprising 4 percent of all African American families in the nation. This small sector of African American families had expanded so rapidly during the 1980s that by 1986, they comprised 9 percent of the total and included some 624,000 families.

One reason for looking at social class stratification is that it helps to show diversity in other dimensions of life, including family structure. Thus,

among the Black upper class, an overwhelming 96 percent are husband-wife families. At a time when it was commonly asserted that 42 percent of all African American families were female-headed families, it is of some consequence to note that only 4 percent of the Black upper class, 17 percent of the middle class, and 40 percent of non-poor working-class families consisted of single parents. Only among the two poor sectors did single-parent families constitute the majority. The impact of social class on family structure is suggested by Table 3.

In sum, socioeconomic class stratification is an important, if often overlooked, dimension of African American family life. A holistic approach that understands the full range of socioeconomic statuses in the Black community can teach all of us the following lessons crucial to the well-being of Black families.

First, it can teach us and our Black children and youth that there is, indeed, room at the top and all along the socioeconomic ladder in legitimate enterprises to challenge and channel all their talents, interests, and abilities.

Children can achieve their aspirations in a wide variety of fields and be rewarded for them if they have the talent, the interest, and the help that they need.

Table 3: African American Social Class and Family Structure

Class	Couple	Parent	Wife
Upper Class	96%	4%	50%
Middle Class	83%	17%	78%
Working Class (Non-poor)	60%	40%	45%
Working Class (Poor)	33%	67%	33%
Underclass (Non-working Poor)	25%	75%	25%

Source: U.S. Bureau of the Census

Second, individual achievement is not incompatible with stable family development, but, instead, the two often go hand-in-hand.

Third, a remarkable concomitant to financial, occupational, and educational success is the ability to make a contribution to others.

Finally, even those with socioeconomic success, who have escaped the worst features of the underclass, still have to fight to overcome injustices and other obstacles unknown to their White counterparts. For those who believe that middle- and upper-class Black families have no problems with racism, a recent study by *Money* magazine should be most instructive. A four-month investigation by *Money* shows in dollars and cents that racial discrimination still prevents middle-class (and upper-class) Black families from earning as much as Whites; lowers their access to mortgages, business loans, and other financial services; retards their home's rate of appreciation; prevents them from increasing their wealth effectively; and deprives them of the economic well being enjoyed by their White middle-class counterparts.

These, then, are insights we gain from understanding African American family diversity that we would never appreciate from a concentration on the Black underclass alone.

CONCLUSION

Generalizations about African American family patterns often degenerate into stereotypes because they fail to put these families in a holistic perspective and understand their complexity and diversity. In their legitimate concern with single-parent families, they fail to appreciate the extent of Black family structural diversity. In their focus on the underclass at the bottom of the socioeconomic scale, they ignore the working class, middle class, and upper class. In their focus on adolescent behavior, including school failure and teen parenting, they ignore important dimensions of the life cycle at younger and older age ranges. Finally, in an often myopic focus on the family as an institution, they ignore its interdependence with the institutional structure of the Black community and with the systems of the larger society. African American family studies urgently need a broader view as urged by DuBois a hundred years ago. Such an approach will help us understand these families better. It will help us to see more clearly their connection with other families. More importantly, it will help us to fashion sounder theories and policies to enhance the structure and the functioning of these families.

NOTES

1. Andrew Billingsley, *Climbing Jacob's Ladder* (New York: Simon and Schuster, 1992).

2. Ibid, p. 207.

3. Ibid.

4. Ibid.

A NATIONAL SURVEY OF AFRICAN AMERICAN PRIESTS AND SEMINARIANS

DR. BERNARD GLOS
REV. EUGENE HEMRICK

The results of the survey are contained in Section A: Demographic Data; Section B: Attitudes, Beliefs, and Experiences; and Section C: Open-Ended Responses.

SURVEY SECTION A: DEMOGRAPHIC DATA

The returned surveys numbered 157. Of these, 89 priests (or 57 percent) identified themselves as affiliated to a diocese, while 68 (or 43 percent) opted for the affiliation of religious order.

The survey asked if the respondent had changed his affiliation at some time. Of those responding, 83 percent indicated that they had never changed their affiliation, while 4 percent began with a diocese and are now with a religious order. Similarly, 13 percent began with a religious order and are now affiliated with a diocese.

Table 1 describes the respondents' current role in the Church.

The mean age (arithmetic average) of respondents was 47.3 years (standard deviation of 13.5, or about two-thirds of the respondents ranged between 33.8 and 60.8 years).

The median age (half the respondents were below and half above this value) was 44. Twelve percent were 30 years of age or younger; 42 percent were between 31 and 45; 26 percent between 46 and 60; and 20 percent were 61 years of age or older. Respondents average 4.64 siblings in their family (median of 4), with 13 percent reporting 8 or more siblings.

Next they were asked to locate their birth order, with "1" being oldest, "2" being second oldest, etc.

Table 1: Current Status

89%	Ordained priest
8%	Seminarian/theology student
3%	College seminarian
0%	Pre-theology program
1%	Novice/pre-novitiate

The mean was 2.98; the median at 2. Thirty-six percent report being the oldest; 15 percent the second oldest; 16 percent the third oldest. It appears that two-thirds of the respondents were from the oldest birth order.

Seventy-seven percent report their mother as Catholic; 61 percent, their father. Nearly all parents were of African American ethnic origin: 96 percent for mothers, 95 percent for fathers.

In terms of the religious affiliation of significant relatives and other individuals in their lives, respondents indicated that slightly less than half, on the average (42.7 percent) were Catholic. The median was 25 percent. Nineteen percent report that 100 percent of significant individuals were Catholic; 26 percent report none were Catholic.

Table 2 presents the family situations during the respondents' childhood years. Two-thirds of respondents indicated that they lived with both natural parents.

Table 3 describes the total family income during respondents' seminary years.

Table 4 presents the highest education level attained by parents.

Louisiana (14 percent), Alabama (8 percent), and Mississippi (11 percent) were most often noted as the mother's place of birth. Louisiana (18 percent), Mississippi (11 percent), and Alabama and Virginia (6 percent each) were most often indicated as the father's place of birth.

Table 5 illustrates the setting in which parents grew up.

Twenty-seven percent of the respondents indicated that their parents were divorced or separated when they entered the seminary. Respondents further indicated that 55.5 percent (mean) of their close friends were Catholic when they were growing up. The median value was 60 percent, with 9 percent indicating

Table 2: Family Situation During Childhood Years

67%	Lived with both natural parents
17%	Lived with mother only
6%	Other
5%	Lived with one natural parent and one step-parent
4%	Lived with family relatives apart from parents
1%	Lived with father only
0%	Lived with older siblings

Table 3: Family Income During Seminary Years

9%	Less than $7,000
25%	$7,000-14,000
17%	$15,000-19,000
19%	$20,000-29,000
16%	$30,000-39,000
14%	Above $40,000

Table 4: Highest Level of Parents' Education

Mother	Father	Educational Level
6%	1%	No formal education
14%	20%	Some elementary school
9%	9%	Elementary school diploma
25%	21%	Some high school
19%	17%	High school diploma/GED
25%	19%	Some college or associate's degree
8%	8%	Bachelor's degree or equivalent
4%	8%	Graduate work/advanced degree

Table 5: Setting in Which Parents Grew up

Mother	Father	Setting
27%	36%	Rural
31%	27%	Small town
6%	6%	Suburban
37%	31%	Urban

none of their close friends were Catholic, 18 percent reporting between 1 and 10 percent, and 11 percent indicating that all of their close friends were Catholic.

Table 6 describes the time of the respondents' baptism.

In terms of racial/ethnic self-descriptors, 52 percent of respondents describe themselves as "African American"; 31 percent as "Black"; and 3 percent each for "African" and "Creole." All other descriptors received a response of 1 percent or less. Table 7 describes the various educational, geographical, and social environments respondents experienced when they were growing up, in terms of racial/ethnic diversity.

In terms of family religious background, 46 percent say that they came from a predominantly Catholic background, 29 percent from a predominantly Protestant or non-Christian background, and 26 percent from a background having mixed religious affiliations.

Table 8 lists respondents' identification of when in their life they first considered a vocation to the priesthood or religious life.

Table 9 shows the relative perceived influence of various individuals, groups, and experiences on the respondents' decision to consider the priesthood. Influences rated more important include one's own prayer and reading, the pastor or parish priest, one's own vision of Church, and family religious life.

Table 6: Time When Respondent Became Catholic

55%	Baptized at birth into Catholic family
24%	Elementary school years
8%	High school years
6%	College years
7%	Other

Table 8: Period of Life When Vocation Was First Considered

39%	Early grade school (grades 1-6)
27%	Junior high (grades 7-8)
18%	High school
9%	College or graduate work
8%	After college or in chosen occupation

Table 7: Racial/Ethnic Diversity of Educational, Geographic, and Social Environments

Scale:
1. Completely or nearly completely non-African American
2. Mostly non-African American
3. Evenly integrated
4. Mostly African American
5. Completely or nearly completely African American

SCALE VALUES					ENVIRONMENT
1	2	3	4	5	
4%	8%	12%	25%	50%	Neighborhood
10%	14%	7%	16%	53%	Elementary school (students)
40%	21%	3%	8%	28%	Elementary school (staff)
32%	26%	10%	7%	25%	High school (students)
54%	22%	8%	5%	11%	High school (staff)
12%	16%	10%	18%	44%	Parish members
82%	10%	4%	1%	3%	Parish clergy
9%	9%	12%	16%	54%	Close friends-grade school
20%	10%	22%	16%	31%	Close friends-high school

Table 9: Influences on Vocational Decision

Data are means (averages) on a seven-point rating scale, with 1 being "not very influential" and 7 being" very influential."

Mean Response	Item	Mean Response	Item
5.66	My own prayer and reading	2.81	Influences of other Catholic families
5.52	Catholic pastor or particular parish priest(s)	2.68	Working in rectory or religious house
5.12	My own vision of church	2.40	Baptismal Godparents
4.90	Family religious life/spirituality	2.09	Diocesan or religious vocation director
4.82	My own involvement in parish activities	2.08	Parish religious education program
4.48	Mother or significant maternal figure	1.86	Older siblings
4.03	Parish life	1.55	Non-Catholic religious experience
4.02	Particular religious education teacher	1.53	Ecumenical activities
3.90	Particular member of religious order	1.36	Volunteer activities (e.g., VISTA)
3.76	Catholic elementary school	1.33	Black Catholic workshops and seminars
3.66	Father or significant paternal figure	1.07	Protestant minister
3.63	Prayer groups or similar activities	1.01	Parish youth ministry
3.63	Particular school teacher	0.99	Particular campus minister
3.35	Grandparents	0.92	College campus ministry
3.33	Catholic high school	0.89	Particular youth minister
3.12	Close personal friend(s)	0.83	Work of Catholic social services
2.89	Other relatives	0.52	RCIA

SURVEY SECTION B: ATTITUDES, BELIEFS, AND EXPERIENCES

Table 10 reports the respondents' evaluation of a set of ministerial priorities. The highest priorities include living one's life in a way that is consistent with Gospel demands and as witness to Jesus Christ; developing one's spiritual life and prayer; preaching and homily preparation; forming community in which people have a sense of mission and belonging; and making the Gospel message regarding the poor, needy, and powerless a major theme of teaching and preaching.

Table 11 illustrates religious practices and how they have changed since entering the seminary or being ordained. Emmaus groups and twelve-step programs are reported most as never having been a part of religious practice. Retreats, liturgical prayer, divine office, and Gospel music show the most increase; meditation, rosary, and devotional books show the most decline.

Table 11: Religious Practices

Percent of respondents in each status category

Key: N-Never a part of my spiritual life
D-Use has declined
S-Use has stayed the same
I-Use has increased

STATUS				PRACTICE
N	D	S	I	
84%	5%	3%	7%	a. Emmaus group
84%	3%	5%	12%	b. Twelve-step program
41%	10%	27%	22%	c. Revival
3%	15%	45%	35%	d. Retreats
26%	25%	29%	19%	e. Prayer group
1%	4%	36%	58%	f. Liturgical prayer
6%	33%	34%	26%	g. Rosary
15%	40%	43%	2%	h. Meditation
2%	22%	41%	35%	I. Divine office
10%	37%	34%	18%	j. Devotional books
14%	12%	21%	52%	k. Gospel music
28%	13%	28%	31%	l. Video/audio tapes
45%	12%	18%	13%	m. Journal writing

Table 10: Ministerial Priorities

Data means from a seven-point rating scale, with 1 being "very low priority" and 7 being "very high priority."

Mean Response	Item
6.50	Living my personal life in a way that is consistent with Gospel demands and as a witness to Jesus Christ
6.31	Developing my own spiritual life and prayer
6.29	Preaching and homily preparation
6.11	Forming a community in which people have a sense of mission and belonging
6.07	Making the Gospel message regarding the poor, needy, and powerless a major theme of my teaching and preaching
6.05	Being the liturgical leader of the community by presiding at the eucharist and other sacraments
5.89	Actively working toward increasing sensitivity to racism in the Church and society
5.72	Catechizing and educating
5.68	Giving spiritual direction and leadership to the parish and individuals within it
5.67	Actively encouraging people to study and pray the scriptures
5.51	Integrating African American religious expression into Catholic worship and prayer
5.42	Increasing my knowledge and skills as a theologian
5.40	Clearly identifying pastoral needs for African American communities
5.40	Creating a parish community where planning and decision making are shared by priests, staff, and people
5.38	Clearly identifying and upholding the Church's traditions and beliefs
5.36	Ministering to bring marginalized individuals into the community through effective evangelization and outreach
5.18	Actively promoting and encouraging vocations to the priesthood and other ministries
5.12	Living a celibate life as a witness to the coming of the Kingdom
5.05	Developing new ministries and structures to more effectively serve the people
4.84	Direct personal ministry to basic human needs, such as food and housing
4.54	Working with community organizations and political groups in social action activities to respond to the basic human needs of good clothing, housing, employment, etc.
4.34	Counseling and advising on nonspiritual matters
4.31	Ministering to the isolated aged
4.27	Coordinating various ministries
4.02	Youth ministry efforts, especially toward gang prevention
3.99	Teaching or other work in high school, college, or seminary
3.98	Ministering with single-parent families
3.97	Working to increase neighborhood safety and reduce same-race crime
3.80	Being an extension of the bishop and representing him to his people
3.78	Working on the problem of drug addiction and drug sales
3.69	Leading retreat programs
3.67	Leading Black Catholic revival
3.60	Home or foreign missionary activity
2.84	Prison ministry
2.49	Being the final authority in the parish on all decisions

In terms of time since entering the seminary or ordination (for those who are ordained) the mean number of years was 18.7. The median response was 15 years. Seventy-eight percent report being affiliated with the National Black Catholic Clergy Caucus. Almost half or 46 percent report being affiliated with a fraternal organization such as Knights of Peter Claver.

Respondents were asked to evaluate their comfort and satisfaction with their vocational choice at this time in their life, using a scale from 1 to 100, with 1 being a total lack of comfort and maximum dissatisfaction, and 100 representing complete comfort and maximum satisfaction. The mean response was 87.50, with the median at 90. Only 6 percent reported a value below 50.

The last item of this section of the survey asked respondents to express agreement or disagreement with a set of statements about the seminary. These are listed in Table 12. The items drawing the greatest agreement have to do with friendship and support, the difficulty of non-African Americans in understanding African American culture, and general improvement in self-concept, comfort in being, and relationships. Least agreement dealt with issues of racially similar personnel and culturally appropriate learning experiences for both African Americans and those of other racial backgrounds.

Table 12: Descriptors of the Seminary and Seminary Life

Data are means from a seven-point rating scale, with 1 indicating "very strongly disagree" and 7, "very strongly agree."

Mean Response	Item
5.81	I have made many friends among seminarians who are not African American.
5.7	My family and friends have always supported my vocational choice.
5.32	Most people here have a difficult time understanding African American culture and people.
5.19	My friends from pre-seminary days have always supported my vocational choice.
5.08	I have increased good feelings about who I am and where I come from and have felt my confidence and self-concept grow.
4.97	I feel very comfortable being an African American here.
4.90	My relationship with my family has improved since I became a seminarian.
4.73	I can relate very well with seminary officials in authority or leadership roles here.
4.69	My family feels comfortable in visiting the seminary.
4.67	The academic courses here appear relevant to my projected needs in the seminary.
4.31	Non-African American seminarians relate well to me and can appreciate my culture.
4.09	There is provision for safely expressing my opinions here.
3.99	I feel comfortable in expressing myself in ways appropriate to my culture and background here.
3.97	There are few things or people who make me feel uncomfortable and second rate.
3.93	I think that other people, too, will regard my race as a plus, rather than a minus.
3.86	The diocesan vocation director or religious formation director has been helpful to me.

Mean Response	Item
3.82	I have come to know my cultural roots better since coming to the seminary.
3.82	I feel a strong need to be academically successful to meet my family expectations.
3.72	I feel that superiors and faculty expect a higher level of performance from African American seminarians than from others.
3.66	I have not felt a sense of separation from my family or background since coming here.
3.64	I sometimes wonder if I will be completely happy as a priest.
3.61	I can expect that my racial background will be an advantage in future dealings with my bishop/superiors.
3.54	Overall, as an African American seminarian, I feel satisfied with the seminary program, personnel, and life.
3.41	I have never felt vulnerable or helpless here.
3.39	I have a difficult time in integrating my spirituality and prayer with the spirituality here.
2.52	The seminary makes efforts to help me understand my roots and culture.
2.49	Adequate practicum or mentoring experiences in the African American community are available here.
2.39	The study of African American history and culture is encouraged for members of other ethnic groups here.
2.31	There has been an emphasis on preparing for African American ministry, even for those seminarians who are not African Americans.
2.30	Food items particular to African American culture appear on the menu here.
1.89	There are enough African American role models here.

SURVEY SECTION C: OPEN-ENDED RESPONSES

Please list the current African American non-theological writers with whom you are familiar.

Names	No. of Responses	Names	No. of Responses	Names	No. of Responses
Baldwin, James	36	Yerby, Frank	2	Toomer, Jean	1
Walker, Alice	32	Steele, Shelby	2	Marable, Manning	1
Morrison, Toni	26	Woodson, Carter G.	2	Kimbroe, Denis	1
Haley, Alex	18	Wilson, August	2	Kajufa, Jawana	1
Angelou, Maya	17	Washington, Mary	2	Phillips, Henry Laird	1
Hughes, Langston	15	Shange, Ntozake	2	Mozley, Walter	1
Wright, Richard	12	Van Sertima, Ivan	2	Perkins, Useni Eugene	1
Davis, Cyprian	12	Cross, William	1	Jones, Dormon	1
Bennett, Lerone	9	Wilson, Dereck	1	Pinkney, Alphonso	1
Giovanni, Nikki	9	Davis, Angela	1	LaPorte, Bryce	1
Malcolm X	8	Diop, Cheikh Anta	1	Perry, Richard	1
DuBois, W. E. B.	7	Plumpp, Sterling	1	Pasteur, Alfred	1
King, Martin Luther	7	Wideman, John E.	1	Lamming, George	1
Franklin, John Hope	6	Crummel, Alexander	1	Nobles, Wade	1
Brooks, Gwendolyn	6	Dukon-Sells, Rose	1	Mamiya, Lawrence H.	1
Ellison, Ralph	6	Wheatley, Phyllis	1	McAdoo, Harriette	1
Madhubuti, Haki R.	5	Frazier, E. Franklin	1	Maalouf, Amin	1
Hurston, Zora Neale	5	Thompson, Farris	1	Lester, Julius	1
Lincoln, C. Eric	5	Walcott, Derek	1	Lee, Hannah	1
Akbar, Naim	5	Wallace, Michelle	1	Levine, Lawrence	1
Asante, Molefi Kete	5	Washington, Booker T.	1	McKay, Claude	1
McMillan, Terry	5	Carey, Lorene	1	Ladner, Joyce A.	1
Douglass, Frederick	4	Evans, Mari	1	Jones, Nathan	1
Raboteau, Albert	4	Edelman, Marian Wright	1	Jones, LeRoy	1
Gates, Henry Louis	4	Comer, James	1	Hill, Paul Jr.	1
Johnson, James Weldon	3	Gill, Walter	1	Harper, Toni	1
Naylor, Gloria	3	Alexander, M. W.	1	Stack, Shelby	1
Williams, Richard	3	Andrews, William	1	Hare, Nathan	1
Bowman, Thea	3	Blassingame, John	1	Hall, Nathaniel B.	1
Pouissant, Alvin	3	Baker	1	Gregory, Dick	1
Gaines, Ernest	3	Wright, Nathan Jr.	1	Gresson, Aaron	1
Walker, Margaret	3	Yee, Shirley J.	1	Giddings, Paula	1
Harding, Vincent	3	Wolfe, George	1	Thurman, Howard	1
Staples, Robert	3	Baldwin, Charles	1	Dunbar, Paul Lawrence	1
Billingsley, Andrew	2	Wyatt	1	Holland, Spencer	1
Browder, Anthony	2	Welsing, Frances	1	Raspberry, William	1
Garvey, Marcus	2	Baraka, Amiri	1	James, C. L. R.	1
Kunjufu, Jawanza	2	Clarke, John Hendrick	1	Johnson, Charles	1
Lee, Don L.	2	Wilkins, Gail	1	ben-Jochannan, Yosef	1
Cruse, Harold	2	Cobbs	1	Jean, Doris	1
Karenga, Ron	2	Brown, Tony	1	Holly, James Theodore	1
Keenan, Randall	2	Christian, Robert	1	Hemphill, Essex	1
Knight, Ethridge	2	Bello, Saul	1	Rogers, J. A.	1
Cone, James	2	Branch, Taylor	1	James, George	1
Karenga, Maulana	2	Brown, Joseph	1		
Hilliard, Asa G. III	2	Daniel, Jack L.	1		

Please list current theological African American writers with whom you are familiar.

Names	No. of Responses	Names	No. of Responses	Names	No. of Responses
Cone, James	72	Massingale, Bryan	2	Gregory, Wilton	1
Braxton, Edward	36	Ela, Jean Marc	2	Grantin	1
Davis, Cyprian	35	Brown, Joseph	2	Grant, Jacquelyn	1
Felder, Cain Hope	22	Arinze, Francis	2	Gilmore, Gayraud	1
Phelps, Jamie	18	Young, Josiah U.	1	Giles, Anthony	1
Wilmore, Gayraud	15	Wright, Nathan Jr.	1	Forbes, James	1
Roberts, DeOtis	12	Wright, Harold L.	1	Fisher, Carl	1
King, Martin Luther	10	Watley, William D.	1	Edwards, Herbert O.	1
Thurman, Howard	9	Walker, Wyatt T.	1	Doohan, Leonard	1
Hayes, Diana	8	Walker, Addie	1	Dennis, Walter D.	1
Copeland, Shawn	8	Tutu, Desmond	1	Dade, Malcolm G.	1
West, Cornel	7	Toldson, Ivery L.	1	Copher, Charles	1
Mitchel, Henry	7	St. Augustine	1	Cooper, Austin	1
Lincoln, C. Eric	7	Smith, J. Alfred Sr.	1	Conwill, Giles	1
Lyke, James	6	Rowe, Cyprian	1	Cobb, John	1
Jones, Major	5	Rivers, Clarence	1	Caution, Tollie L.	1
Bowman, Thea	4	Reems	1	Burgess, John M.	1
Moyd, Olin	3	Raboteau, Albert	1	Boesak, Allan (South African)	1
Mbiti, John	3	Proctor	1	Bennet	1
Cleage, Albert B.	3	Pasteur, Alfred	1	Behm, Ronald	1
Carter, Junius F.	3	Miller, George Frazier	1	Barrett, Leonard	1
Witvliet, Theo	2	McKnight, A. J.	1	Banks, William L.	1
Weems, Renita	2	Malcolm X	1	Akbar, N'aim	1
Washington, Joseph D.	2	Lawson, James	1	Abrani, Bede	1
Smithson, Sandra O.	2	Kunjufu, Jawanza	1	Salley, Columbus	1
Murray, J. Glenn	2	Jordan, Theodus J.	1		

What three magazines do you read the most?

Names	No. of Responses	Names	No. of Responses	Names	No. of Responses
Ebony	60	Black Enterprise	2	Plain Truth	1
Time	42	Architectural Digest	2	People	1
Newsweek	42	Yale Alumni Magazine	1	Omni	1
America	21	World Report	1	New York Times Magazine	1
Jet	17	Word Among Us	1	New York Review of Books	1
National Catholic Reporter	9	West Africa	1	National Black Review	1
Priest	8	Voice	1	Missiology	1
Origins	7	Venture Inward	1	Men's Fitness	1
American Visions	7	Vanity Fair	1	Maryknoll	1
U.S. Catholic	6	Utne Reader	1	Lancet	1
Essence	6	Twin Circle	1	Journal of Feminist Studies in Religion	1
Emerge	6	Today's Parish	1	Journal of Religious Thought	1
U.S. News	5	Today's Priest	1	Josephite Harvest	1
Sojourners	5	This Rock	1	Homiletic & Pastoral Review	1
National Geographic	5	The American	1	Harpers	1
Ebony Man	5	The Village Voice	1	Forum	1
Money	4	The Jurist	1	First Things	1
Modern Liturgy	4	The Month	1	Fidelity	1
Commonweal	4	The New Republic	1	Faith and Formation	1
Chicago Studies	4	The Church Today	1	Esquire	1
Theological Studies	3	Tennis	1	Education	1
New Yorker	3	Tablet	1	Columbian	1
Gentlemen's Quarterly	3	St. Augustine Catholic	1	Claverite	1
Crisis	3	St. Anthony Messenger	1	Catholic World Report	2
Catholic Digest	3	Spiritual Life	1	Catholic International	1
Black Scholar	3	Speculum: Journal of Medical Studies	1	Catholic Historical Review	2
Worship	2	Southern Living	1	Catholic Answer	1
Theology Digest	2	Southern Exposure	1	Catholic Register	1
Sports Illustrated	2	Soul	1	Catholic Theological Review	1
Parabola	2	Smithsonian	1	Black Issues in Higher Education	1
New Oxford Review	2	Review for Religious	1	Audio	1
New Covenant	2	Religions Teacher Journal	1	African Ecclesial Review	1
Life	2	Priests and People	1	African American Visions	1
Entertainment Weekly	2	Priestly Ministry	1	30 Days	1
Church	2	Post	1		

What kind of music do you like to
listen to? (first preference listed)

What are your favorite recreational activities?

NAMES	NO. OF RESPONSES
Classical	46
Gospel	23
Jazz	19
All	7
Religious	6
Pop	5
Opera	4
Rhythm and blues	3
Easy listening	3
Soul	2
Gregorian chant	2
FM instrumentals	2
Country	2
Broadway musicals	2
Renaissance	1
Reggae	1
Rap	1
PBS	1
None	1
New age	1
Light rock	1
James Brown	1
Good music	1
Calypso	1

NAMES	NO. OF RESPONSES
Sports/athletics	78
Reading	45
Walking	30
Music	25
Films	19
Exercising	19
Traveling	16
Theater	16
Watching television	15
Socializing	10
Cooking	8
Outdoor activities	7
Musical instruments	7
Dance	5
Attending/watching athletic events	5
Writing	4
Water activities	4
Singing	4

NAMES	NO. OF RESPONSES
Games	4
Dining	4
Gardening	3
Art appreciation	3
Youth programs	2
Shopping	2
Plants	2
Photography	2
Hobby trains	2
Aquarium fish raising	2
Working	1
Stamp collecting	1
Quiet time alone	1
Parades	1
Historical research	1
Flying	1
Computers	1
Beautifying church interior	1

Please indicate reasons why former seminarians/priests that you knew left.

DESCRIPTION	NO. OF RESPONSES
Celibacy/sexuality	53
Disagreements/frustration with the Church or authority figures in the Church	51
Decided it was not the life for them	44
Racism	33
Lack of support/appreciation	30
Marriage/family life/outside relationships	28
Personal shortcomings	22
Lack of cultural fit/support	14
Burnout	10
Family obligations	2

What can the Church do to attract more African Americans to the priesthood?

DESCRIPTION	NO. OF RESPONSES
Include more African American culture in the services, curriculum, vocational materials, etc.	37
Put more Blacks in authority/high visibility positions	33
Actively recruit African American candidates	22
Provide encouragement, appreciation, and support to Blacks within the Church	21
Actively combat racism in the Church, seminaries, and society	17
Be truly Christian/Catholic	11
Educate all current Catholic leadership and parishioners in multicultural awareness	10
Allow sexuality and family life for priests	9
Speak more to issues of the Black community	8
Special programs, such as a weekend experience for young Black males, more emphasis on secular campuses, separate communities of African American religious, inviting Black youth to pre-vocation days, Catholic conference for African Americans	7
Strengthen family and community life, spiritually and emotionally	5
Good Catholic teaching from elementary school on in Black communities	4

DESCRIPTION	NO. OF RESPONSES
Provide financial support for under-privileged students	4
Pray	3
Listen to youth and offer them more	3
Ask current clergy, bishops, and vocation directors what prevents recruitment of Blacks	3
Advertise showing African American Catholics	3
Treat African American priests and parishioners the same as White ones	2
Work with parents to encourage vocations in their children	1
The bishops must lead the effort	1
The Church needs to be more specific/clear in its theology	1
Strengthen urban ministry	1
Promotion of deacons	1
Present it as a spiritual call	1
More genuineness, commitment, and happiness of priests	1
Mention need for priests everywhere we go	1
Look at the success of the Muslims	1
Keep churches open in Black communities	1
Involve laity in recruitment	1
Improve conditions in which African American priests must live and serve	1
Improve our image and credibility	1
Discard polygenesis and race consciousness	1
Assign Blacks to all kinds of parishes, not just Black	1

When asked, **"What has been your greatest joy in studying for/being a priest?"** the responses grouped into four major categories (listed in order of decreasing frequency):

(1) Enjoying a particular aspect of ministry
(2) Some type of personal gain
(3) Service
(4) A racial/cultural experience

Typical examples of each type of response:

1. Enjoying a particular aspect of ministry
- Liturgical ministry/sacramental ministry
- Parish work
- Deepening one's insights in theology and scripture
- The beauty of ordination in itself
- Ministering to/with youth
- Teaching

2. Some type of personal gain
- Self-fulfillment
- Discovering myself in relationship to Jesus Christ
- Meeting great people
- Continual development of my prayer life and closeness to God
- Intellectual development

3. Service
- Being there for those who may need my help
- Helping people to a deeper awareness of God's presence in their lives
- Knowing that I can make a difference
- Supporting people in taking control of their lives

4. A racial/cultural experience
- Knowing that there are other African American seminarians struggling like myself/solidarity
- Learning and growing in my identity as an African American
- Meeting other Black brothers and sisters who are walking the same road I'm walking
- Celebrating eucharist in an African American parish setting which has become an extended family for all, especially African American Catholics
- Experiencing different cultures proclaiming the good news

When asked, **"What has been your greatest sorrow in studying for/being a priest?"**, answers range among five general topics. They are listed here in order of decreasing frequency with examples of actual responses.

1. Experiencing racism, lack of appreciation for African American culture, stereotyping, and/or cultural isolation
- Lack of understanding or respect for other cultures in the Church
- Separated from the African American community
- Racism exhibited by priests and seminarians
- Being branded as a radical whenever African Americans speak out
- Experiencing rejection by my own people who have internalized self-hatred
- Having no courses in African American studies
- The Church's seemly loss of interest in civil rights
- No opportunity to get beyond stereotypes
- Experiencing persons dropping out because of race
- The low priority African American and inner-city problems receive from diocesan officials
- Not having African American priests as role models

2. A personal weakness, problem, or loss
- Loss of friends in the priesthood
- Financial problems
- Leaving family
- Not having a family of my own
- Loneliness
- Personal weaknesses and failures
- Wishing to become a priest sooner
- Burnout

3. A particular aspect of the job or seminary experience
- Not being effective at turning souls to the Lord
- Very little time for reading and relaxation
- Dealing with tragedies of others
- The difficulty with vocation recruitment
- Administrative duties
- Writing term papers

4. Disagreement or frustration with the Church and/or its leaders
- Seeing good men kicked out of the seminary for the wrong reasons and seeing unhealthy men permitted to stay and be ordained

- The collaborative method of running parishes
- Too often talking around the real issues that could have made us more critical thinkers and more responsive ministers
- Poor leadership
- Hearing stories of priests and fellow religious scandalizing the faithful by the way they conduct their lives
- Post Vatican II revisionism
- The Church's attitude towards sex

5. Feeling unsupported, unappreciated, and/or disrespected

- Public attack on the Church/priesthood
- Lack of support or challenge in my personal development
- A disrespect and devaluing of my gifts
- Hardness of heart and lack of spiritual leadership by superiors
- Wanting a deeper experience of community and fraternity among priests

When asked, **"What, if any, changes would you recommend for seminary formation programs?"**, four basic categories of suggestions dealing with content, inculturation, leadership, and structure surfaced.

1. Content suggestions

- Include African American studies in all seminaries.
- Emphasize love and oneness in the Catholic Church of Christ.
- Include courses in sociology of religion, Spanish, intracultural awareness, administration, prayer and spirituality, exorcism, history, Latin, Greek, counseling, homiletics, 12-step programs, liturgical practice, physical education, leadership, sacred music, sexuality, economics, political science.
- Put more emphasis on grass roots experience.
- Teach more critical thinking.
- Be more loyal to the pope.
- Concentrate on full and healthy personality development to face a tough, complex world.
- Emphasize scripture personally and pastorally.

2. Inculturation suggestions

- Provide more cultural diversity and sensitivity.
- Dialogue between cultures in order to look not only at differences but at similarities as well.
- Include more field experience in the African American community.

- Actively assist Black students to identify themselves in the context of the paschal mystery.
- Stop requiring African Americans to become Eurocentric.
- Deal with racism/hold racism conferences.
- Have even expectations and opportunities for everyone.

3. Leadership suggestions

- Have professors who are more human, sensitive, compassionate, and closer to Jesus.
- Appoint a multicultural staff and faculty.
- Eliminate misfits in the direction and teaching staff.
- Provide mentors that understand the seminarian and where he is coming from, especially the socioeconomic background.
- Give seminarians more on-the-job training with priests who care and love.

4. Structural suggestions

- Give seminarians time with the people.
- Get rid of formal college and high school seminaries.
- Have a program for African Americans.
- Let married deacons go on studying for the priesthood.
- Send all students from different communities to a big seminary to live and study.
- Remove religious orders from the training of diocesan priests.
- Remove women from priestly formation.
- Put African Americans in clusters for support.
- Close the "Big Houses."
- Move towards a university or professional education model.
- Take only candidates from military institutions after successful accomplishment there and militarize the seminary itself.
- Expand contact with other students, including females, not seeking ordination.
- Provide an opportunity for African American seminarians to come together by themselves once in a while.
- Repeal celibacy.

What, if any, changes would you recommend for seminary formation programs?

Description	No. of Responses
More cultural diversity and sensitivity in curriculum/liturgy/interaction/environment	44
More African American faculty/staff/mentors/role models	23
Give seminarians time with the people in the African American community	14
Courses on prayer/spirituality/liturgy/doctrine	6
Better role models in professors/staff	5
Teach administration/finances/facilities management	4
Concentrate on overall healthy mind/personality development	3
Students live within a parish family while in school	2
More critical thinking	2
Expand contact with students not seeking ordination	2
Emphasis on love and openness	2
Deal with racism	2
Courses in counseling	2
Cluster African American students for support either within a seminary or in periodic gatherings across seminaries	2
A separate program for African Americans	2
Willingness to search for new models of formation	1
Train for urban ministry	1
Students must take responsibility for their own formation	1

Description	No. of Responses
Stress community prayer	1
Separate training of religious orders from diocesan priests	1
Repeal celibacy	1
Professional education model vs. "Big House"	1
Physical education for mind-body synthesis	1
No women	1
More pastoral innovation and theological fidelity	1
Less emphasis on non-clerical training	1
Leadership courses	1
Help Black students identify with paschal mystery	1
Faculty/staff emphasis on prayer, not politics	1
Equal expectations/opportunities for all	1
Emphasis on working with laity	1
Eliminate high school and college seminaries	1
Courses in Latin and Greek	1
Course in sacred music	1
Course in sexuality	1
Course in politics/economics	1
Course on exorcism	1
Clearer priestly identity	1
Be more loyal to the pope	1
All types of students to one big seminary	1

A COMMENTARY ON THE NATIONAL SURVEY OF AFRICAN AMERICAN PRIESTS AND SEMINARIANS

REV. JOHN FORD

Our joint hands raised houseposts of trust that withstand the siege of envy and the termites of time. (Wole Soyinka, *Death and The Kings*)

It is something of a truism in psychology that if you are treated consistently in a certain way, you eventually internalize that as representing who you are. Although the survey on African American seminarians and priests was not intended to delve into psychodynamic issues, it is not inappropriate to wonder whether these survey results provide a clear indication as to how African American priests and seminarians feel they have been treated. In addition, can we assume that what these men have internalized is representative of who they are?

Each of these men brings a unique richness to the Church that is not immediately apparent in their responses. However, three things are apparent: (1) this is not a homogeneous group; (2) in terms of age, the majority of the men are at the peak of their creativity and generativity; and (3) there is no guarantee that this sampling represents either the total number of African American priests and seminarians or the distinctive geographic regions of the nation from which they originate.

What can we infer about these men? Judging from their ministerial priorities, it would appear that African American priests and seminarians have indeed internalized an identifiable sense of priesthood for themselves. But it is an uneven mixture of cultic, community-building, and justice-oriented styles of priesthood that informs that identity. At first glance, there are no significant or compelling indications that the respondents' priorities are any different from those of their White counterparts.

In a similar fashion, an open-ended question sought to discover "What has been your greatest joy in studying for or being a priest?" Out of the four major categories that emerged, racial and/or cultural experience is the last response in order of decreasing frequency. And, prescinding from the use of Gospel music as a part of one's spirituality, there appears to be nothing distinctly African American about their personal religious practices.

The expectation might have been that this survey would show that all African American priests and seminarians are qualitatively different from those of other racial and ethnic groups. Certainly the decades of the 1960s and 1970s held out the expectation that African American priests would make a difference, be culturally competent in ministering to their own people, not lead sheltered lives, and not retreat into piety when racism and its trauma demanded remedy.

But this survey may point to two unsettling realities: First, the expectations that have been placed upon African American priests and seminarians (in contrast to priests from other ethnic groups) may be naive and wishful. Second, whether an African American is involved in the corporate world or the institutional Church, there is a certain persona (generally, the mirror image of Whites in authority) that must be intentionally developed and cultivated in order to be accepted, to survive, or to succeed. In this process, certain aspects of one's personal sense of self have to be denied. According to one African American corporate executive, any expression of his blackness was perceived as a threat to the corporation's purpose and image. As a result, he safeguarded his career and excelled at his work because of his ability "to sit on [his] contained rage."

Is there a parallel process occurring in the Church among African American priests and seminarians? Probably. For, on the one hand, the respondents convey a remarkable level of comfort in terms of seminary life, while, on the other hand, a type of cultural imperative dominates their responses to questions related to structural change, vocational recruitment, and personal sorrows.

Moreover, the respondents' call for African American mentors and role models seems almost poignant. This is the sense when one considers that 84 percent of the respondents first considered priesthood before their completion of high school; the majority of the respondents entered the seminary at the median age of 15. At that age, individuals require certain kinds of personal contacts as a function of human development; the evolution of emotional independence from one's family of origin is at stake; there is an effort to form one's identity; and there is a need for a significant figure who can serve as a model to emulate. Against this background, the seminary could have provided the context in which to negotiate both personal contacts and emotional independence from family. Be that as it may, it should be noted that the most visible and available role models and mentors for the respondents were probably White priests and religious.

It is unfortunate that this survey instrument cannot gauge the degree to which the quality of that earlier mentoring may have eventuated into identification with White priests and religious and the cultural and religious values they symbolized. Understanding the power of such a possible identification would begin to reveal whether

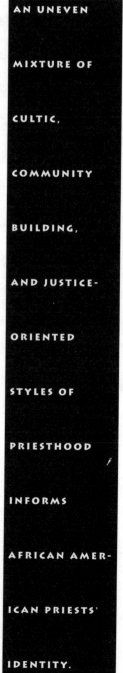

AN UNEVEN MIXTURE OF CULTIC, COMMUNITY BUILDING, AND JUSTICE-ORIENTED STYLES OF PRIESTHOOD INFORMS AFRICAN AMERICAN PRIESTS' IDENTITY.

the respondents' call for African American mentors and cultural opportunities is mere rhetoric or a statement of urgent necessity.

Whatever speculations one might offer after examining the results of this national survey, there is an image that comes to mind. It is the image of the bonsai plant—a tree that is dwarfed by the pruning off of its branches, the cutting back of its roots, and its forced acclimation to a pot-bound existence. As remarkable and marvelous as this achievement might be, the natural and emergent potential of the original object has been neutralized.

Does this survey present us with that image— African American priests and seminarians who are remarkable, yet neutralized by pruning, cutting back, containment, and intentional culturing? Hopefully, their present reality is based on a much more germane image:

> Live on in me, as I do in you. No more than a branch can bear fruit of itself apart from the vine, can you bear fruit apart from me. (Jn 15:4)

COMMENTS ON A NATIONAL STUDY OF AFRICAN AMERICAN PRIESTS AND SEMINARIANS

REV. ROLLINS E. LAMBERT

Perhaps the first fact that stands out in reading the survey data is that these men are not "color-blind"; they are very much aware that they are African Americans and that their race has an impact on most aspects of their lives and ministries. Although they are ordained (or preparing to be ordained) for a priesthood which is universal, capable of providing the services of the Catholic Church to people of any race, color, or nationality, that priesthood is exercised by individuals who were African American before they were priests and will remain African American throughout their ministerial lives. Many or most of them are living with and working for people of similar backgrounds; and those backgrounds may be advantageous or disadvantageous to the work of the Church among these people. It is clear from the responses in the survey that race and racism have been and remain major concerns for the priests and seminarians. They are quite aware that they are living in a society permeated by racism; the Church and its institutions are not immune from this contagious inequality which is backed by centuries of tradition.

The self-descriptors are interesting: the designation *African American* is of recent origin but it has won over a majority of the priests/seminarians. Implied in the use of this designator are a number of items that affect Catholic members of the African American group. Among them:

- Interest in African culture and history.

- Interest in Christianity as it existed and still exists among non-Catholics; especially important here are the musical and preaching traditions that may have some African roots but which developed in the slavery and post-slavery life of African Americans. It is reflected

RACE AND RACISM HAVE BEEN AND REMAIN MAJOR CONCERNS FOR THE PRIESTS AND SEMINARIANS.

in the interest of priests and seminarians in "Gospel music" and a worship style that contains some of these elements.

Growing up and being educated in a system that does not provide role models in African American men, priests or laymen, is a problem reflected in several ways in the responses. School integration was for a long time a primary objective of the civil rights movement; its success is evident in the data, but the data also reveal that African American students generally attend elementary and high schools with predominantly White staffs. One wonders about the effect of having few if any African American teachers, advisors, and mentors in the educational system. The same lacuna appears in the data on seminary life. What happens to African American cultural and traditional values in such a situation? The men look for them in the seminary and find them absent. The burden of providing them rests on the family, the African American community, and perhaps the Church.

RECRUITMENT

The data on recruitment of seminarians and the early influences promoting a vocation are interesting: they indicate that the programmatic search for vocations operative in many dioceses and religious orders is futile where African American youth are concerned. Far more important are one-on-one contacts with priests. Given the fact that it is usually the younger clergy who relate well to young people, the future is not promising: young priests are becoming scarcer. (This lack is not specific to African American Catholics: the absence of young priests is universal in the United States.) From the data, it appears that group associations, vocation directors, religious education programs, volunteer activities, and the like are far less effective in recruitment than the personal influence of a priest. Perhaps it is relevant to mention here that many priests are becoming wary of such one-on-one contact with young people, following the recent scandals of clergy child abuse. This presents a serious dilemma to many priests.

PRIORITIES

Looking at the ministerial priorities, one might be surprised at the absence of ecumenical activity. The survey does not suggest reasons for this absence. One might surmise that the respondents are so preoccupied with pastoral care of the Catholic flock that no time or energy remains for ecumenism. Moreover, Catholic parishes are often regarded with suspicion by Protestant clergy as potential competition or proselytizing raiders of their congregations. The lack of enthusiasm may not be entirely on the Catholic side.

One might also regret that prison ministry comes in as a very low priority. This is an extremely difficult ministry, but given the large number of African American men in U.S. prisons, it would seem that an important opportunity for evangelization is being missed or overlooked. The Muslims are neither missing nor overlooking it.

The development of lay leadership, the spiritual formation of the laity, and the development of real community are high among the priorities listed. This can be a very hopeful sign, provided that such leadership is not restricted to "Church" affairs. It is important where the internal affairs of the parish and the diocese are concerned, but it must not be forgotten that Vatican II insisted that the mission of the laity is to be leaven in the larger society. The leadership developed should also be prepared to function in political, economic, and social life, whether locally, nationally, or even internationally.

RELIGIOUS PRACTICES

Seventy-eight percent of the respondents indicated affiliation with the National Black Catholic Clergy Caucus (NBCCC). The NBCCC has a great potential for good among the African American clergy, but it has not been adequately developed, probably for lack of full-time personnel. The existing staff consists of priests and religious men who have full-time ministries. A more effective NBCCC could provide a support system, especially for men working in isolation from other African American clergy/seminarians. It could provide for the exchange of ideas as well as personal supportive friendships. The NBCCC does hold annual meetings, which are necessary and well-planned. But such meetings have limitations: there is a mix of priests, religious men and women, and seminarians. This is not conducive to in-depth study. Moreover, the diversity of situations in which African American priests work calls for regional analysis and planning. Such activity on the part of the NBCCC, nationally or regionally, could also deal with the disagreements and frustrations with church authorities that are high among the reasons why priests/seminarians left the priesthood or seminary.

EXPECTATIONS FOR THE FUTURE

1. Recruitment of young men into seminaries will become more difficult in the future as the African American clergy grow older and are not replaced by younger men. It seems a universal fact of life that younger priests deal most effectively with youth and provide them with both counseling and role models. The influence of Catholic schools has been small in this regard and, as the number of parochial elementary schools declines, so will that small influence.

2. The demand for a married priesthood, already widespread in Catholic circles, will receive substantial support from African American seminarians and priests. The only mention of permanent deacons who may be married and can offer substantial help in parish ministry comes, in the survey, with the suggestion that deacons be ordained priests after further study.

3. Recruiting seminarians and keeping them on the track to priesthood will depend on their being provided with relevant African American study, and contact with other African American seminarians and with African American laity.

4. The real or apparent neglect of African American communities and their problems with bishops/religious superiors is an impediment to both evangelization in general and recruitment of African American clergy. Strong leadership must be provided to counter this perception by seminarians, priests, and laity.

SUMMARY

The survey reveals no surprises, no shocking new insights, but it does underline what all African American people in the United States have known all along: that racism is a factor that taints even the best-intentioned efforts of church authorities to evangelize African American people. The survey emphasizes, too, that race and culture are essential elements in the lives of African American clergy and laity. To ignore them imperils even the best efforts of White clergy, religious, and laity who work in an African American community. While race and African American culture may be seen as obstacles to the growth of a Church that is universal, these elements may be viewed more fruitfully as manifestations of the beautiful variety of God's people, enriching the whole Church.

GROWING UP AND BEING EDUCATED IN A SYSTEM THAT DOES NOT PROVIDE ROLE MODELS IN AFRICAN AMERICAN MEN IS A PROBLEM.

A NATIONAL STUDY OF AFRICAN AMERICAN PERMANENT DEACONS

DR. BERNARD GLOS
REV. EUGENE HEMRICK

The study of African American permanent deacons is divided into three sections: Section A: Demographic Data; Section B: Attitudes, Beliefs, and Experiences; and Section C: Open-Ended Questions.

Out of approximately 300 African American permanent deacons, 99 returned the survey.

SURVEY SECTION A: DEMOGRAPHIC DATA

The average age of African American deacons is 59 years old and ranges between 34 and 87 years old. Deacons average 8.7 years in ministry since being ordained. Table 1 describes the Catholic/African American roots of deacons.

Table 1: Catholic/African American Roots

Mother	Catholic	58%
Father	Catholic	44%
Mother	African American	96%
Father	African American	95%

Table 2 reflects the time at which African American deacons were baptized.

Thirty-six percent of deacons say they grew up with no Catholic relatives or friends; 17 percent report that all their relatives and friends were Catholic. The average number of Catholic relatives or friends with whom deacons grew up is 42 percent.

Almost all (92 percent) of deacons' wives are Catholic; 91 percent are African American.

Table 3 reflects the various educational, geographical, and social environments deacons experienced while growing up and after ordination in terms of ethnic diversity.

Table 2: Time of Baptism

Baptized at birth	46%
In elementary school	17%
In high school	9%
In college years	7%
After college years	20%

Table 3: Racial/Ethnic Diversity of Educational, Geographic, and Social Environments

	Completely/ Nearly non-African American	Mostly non-African American	Evenly Integrated	Mostly African American	Completely/ Nearly African American	Does Not Pertain
Neighborhood	3%	9%	11%	33%	44%	—
Elementary school students	4	9	6	24	56	1
Elementary school staff	25	11	4	14	43	2
High school students	6	16	5	13	58	1
High school staff	22	18	6	10	41	2
Parish members	12	13	10	28	32	4
Parish clergy	60	24	5	4	3	3
Close friends in college/university	8	19	17	20	30	7
Close friends after ordination	7	9	43	28	11	1

Table 4: Family of Origin: Denomination Background

Predominately Catholic background	36%
Mixed religious affiliation	25%
Protestant/non-Christian background	38%

Table 5: Economic Background

Less than $7,000	0%
$7,000-14,999	3%
$15,000-19,999	2%
$20,000-29,999	12%
$30,000-39,999	19%
Above $40,000	63%

Table 6: Educational Background

No formal education	0%
Some elementary school	10
Elementary school diploma	0
Some high school	2
High school diploma/GED	8
Some college or associate's degree	26
Bachelors or equivalent	20
Graduate work/advanced degree	43

Table 4 reflects the original denominational background of African American deacons.

Table 5 reports the economic background of deacons.

Table 6 describes the educational background of deacons.

Home Setting. Sixty-two percent grew up in an urban setting; 20 percent in a small town; 13 percent in a rural area, and 4 percent in a suburb. Presently 56 percent live in an urban setting; 28 percent in the suburbs; 13 percent in a small town; and 3 percent in a rural area.

Marital Status. Ninety percent are married; 5 percent widowed; 3 percent never married, and 2 percent are divorced or separated.

Family Vocations. Almost all deacons (99 percent) have had no children enter the religious life.

Personal Vocation. Sixty percent say that they once considered a vocation to the priesthood or brotherhood.

Ministerial Stability. Most African American deacons (88 percent) have served in one diocese only, 10 percent served in two dioceses, and 2 percent served in four dioceses.

Affiliations. Better than two-thirds (68 percent) belong to the National Black Catholic Clergy Caucus, and 53 percent report belonging to fraternal organizations like the Knights of Peter Claver and Knights of Columbus.

SURVEY SECTION B: ATTITUDES, BELIEFS, AND EXPERIENCES

On a scale of 1 to 7, with 1 being a very low priority and 7 being a very high priority, deacons reflect the following attitudes on practicing their ministry (Table 7).

Table 7: Ministerial Priorities

6.7	Living my personal life in a way that is consistent with Gospel demands and as a witness to Jesus Christ.
6.3	Developing my own spiritual life and prayer.
6.2	Making the Gospel message regarding the poor, needy, and powerless a major theme of my teaching and preaching.
6.1	Increasing my knowledge and skills as a deacon.
5.9	Actively working toward increasing sensitivity to racism in the Church and society.
5.8	Clearly identifying and upholding the Church's traditions and beliefs.
5.7	Preaching and homily preparation.
5.6	Creating a parish community where planning and decision making are shared by priests, deacons, staff, and people.
5.5	Forming a community in which people have a sense of mission and belonging.
5.5	Actively encouraging people to study and pray the scripture.
5.5	Catechizing and educating.
5.5	Giving spiritual direction and leadership to the parish and individuals within it.
5.3	Clearly identifying pastoral needs for African American communities.
5.3	Pastoral care of the sick.
5.2	Ministering to bring marginalized individuals into the community through effective evangelization and outreach.
5.2	Integrating African American religious expression into Catholic worship and prayer.
5.0	Being a para-liturgical leader of the community by presiding at the sacraments.
4.9	Direct personal ministry to basic human needs, such as food, housing, etc.
4.8	Actively promoting and encouraging vocations to the priesthood and other ministries.
4.8	Reaching out to the isolated aged.
4.7	Being an extension of the bishop and representing him to the people.
4.7	Working with community organizations and political groups in social action activities to respond to the basic human needs of good clothing, housing, employment, etc.
4.6	Developing new ministries and structures to more effectively serve the people.
4.4	Working to increase neighborhood safety and reduce same-race crime.
4.3	Counseling and advising on non-spiritual matters.
4.1	Youth ministry efforts, especially toward gang prevention.
3.9	Leading Black Catholic Revival.
3.8	Working on the problem of drug addiction and drug sales.
3.8	Ministering with single-parent families.
3.7	Leading retreat programs.
3.6	Prison ministry.
3.6	Coordinating various ministries.
3.1	Teaching or other work in high school, college, or seminary.
3.0	Home or foreign missionary activity.

Table 8: Spiritual Practices

	Never Part of my Spiritual Life	Use Has Declined	Use Has Stayed Same	Use Has Increased
Emmaus group	91%	2%	5%	2%
Twelve-step program	81	6	8	6
Revival	17	10	44	28
Retreats	1	6	31	61
Prayer group	6	23	30	40
Liturgical prayer	4	2	33	60
Rosary	6	20	37	35
Meditation	3	39	56	0
Divine office	15	8	28	4
Devotional books	5	16	34	44
Gospel music	12	2	40	44
Video/audio tapes	17	10	32	41
Journal writing	52	14	26	8

Table 8 reflects the increase or decrease in certain spiritual exercises deacons practice.

African American theological writers deacons are most familiar with include the following:

James Cone	21
Cyprian Davis	18
Cain Hope Felder	11
Edward Braxton	10
Jamie Phelps	7
Thea Bowman	6
Eric C. Lincoln	5
Martin Luther King	4
Clarence Williams	4

(The list includes those mentioned four or more times. The number next to the author is the number of times mentioned by deacons.)

African American non-theological writers deacons are most familiar with include:

Maya Alexander	13
James Baldwin	13
Alex Haley	13
Lerone Bennet	11
Alice Walker	8
Cyprian Davis	7
Martin Luther King	5
Richard Wright	5
Web DuBois	5
Langston Hughes	4
Toni Morrison	4

Magazines most read:

Ebony	33
Time	20
Deacon Digest	17
Newsweek	11
Catholic Digest	10
Jet	10
Readers Digest	9
Liguorian	7
America	5
Essence	5
Black Enterprise	4
Homiletic Pastoral Review	4
National Geographic	4

Music most listened to:

Jazz	40
Gospel	37
Classical	33
Blues	15
Popular/contemporary	13

Religious	10
Country	6
Rhythm	5
Western	4
Oldies	4

Favorite recreational activities:

Walking/jogging	26
Reading	24
Watching T.V./sports	23
Fishing	17
Golf	12
Swimming	11
Travel	8
Bowling	8
Listening to music	8
Tennis	6
Camping	5
Hunting/target shooting	5
Theater	4
Gardening	4
Basketball	4

On a scale of 1 to 7, with 1 signifying strong disagreement and 7, strong agreement, deacons reflect their attitudes toward their diaconal ministry.

6.6	My family feels comfortable with me being a deacon.
6.4	My family and friends have always supported my vocational choice.
6.3	I feel very comfortable among my peers being an African American.
6.3	I have not felt a sense of separation from my family or background since becoming a deacon.
6.2	I can relate well with church officials in authority or leadership roles.
6.1	I feel comfortable in expressing myself in ways appropriate to my culture and background as a deacon.
6.1	My friends have always supported my vocational choice.
5.8	My relationship with my family has improved since I became a deacon.
5.6	I have increased in good feelings about who I am and where I come from, and have felt my confidence and self-concept grow since being a deacon.
5.5	Non-African American deacons/priests relate well to me and can appreciate my culture.
5.5	I have made many friends among deacons who are not African American.
5.5	There is provision for safely expressing my opinions as a deacon.
5.5	The academic courses I receive appear relevant to my needs in ministry.
5.2	I have never felt vulnerable or helpless as a deacon.
4.9	The diocesan deacon director has been helpful to me.
4.8	I feel a strong need to be academically successful to meet my diaconate expectations.
4.7	Overall, as an African American deacon, I feel satisfied with the diaconate program, personnel, and life.
4.5	I have come to know my cultural roots better since becoming a deacon.
4.5.	Most people among my peers have a difficult time understanding African American culture and people.
4.3	There are few things or people who make me feel uncomfortable or second rate.
4.0	I think that other people, too, regard my race as a plus rather than a minus.
3.9	The study of African American history and culture is encouraged for members of other ethnic groups in the diaconate program.
3.8	I expect that my racial background will be an advantage in future dealings with my bishop/superiors.
3.6	Adequate practicum or mentoring experiences in the African American community are available.
3.0	I feel that superiors expect a higher level of performance from African American deacons than from others.
2.9	I sometimes wonder if I am as happy as I should be as a deacon.
2.9	I have a difficult time integrating my spirituality and prayer into the workplace.
2.7	There has been an emphasis on preparing for African American ministry, even for those deacons who are not African American.
2.1	There are enough African American role models in the diaconate.

SURVEY SECTION C: OPEN-ENDED RESPONSES

When asked about their comfort and satisfaction at this time with their vocational choice on a scale of 1 to 100, with 100 meaning total satisfaction and comfort, deacons average 89 percent on the scale, indicating great satisfaction.

When asked, "What most inspired you to consider the diaconate?", 27 deacons said they wanted "to serve others/the Church/Christ," and 18 said they were "asked by the pastor/priest/friends." Other reasons given included:

Impressed with the Catholic religion.

Information from a friend and an interview with the program (diaconate) director, prayer, and reflection.

My work in my parish as a lector, etc.

When I met an African American deacon, I became more interested and committed to an ordained ministry. I had already become an active lay minister.

After retiring from the military I was inspired by a deacon I'd met. His work started me.

A group of deacons came to our parish and spoke to us on the diaconate program.

Recommendation of parish staff.

More independent and free to marry.

The Holy Spirit's guidance.

I had been working with the St. Vincent de Paul Society and priests. They invited me to think about the diaconate. I had two brothers who had become permanent deacons. They said, "Since you are already doing the work of a deacon, you should study and become one with us." Then, my wife and I visited St. Joseph's in Montreal,

Canada, and Notre Dame, where we prayed. It was then that I asked God to guide me in what he wanted me to do in my retirement years.

The example of several religious sisters and priests I knew as a child and young adult. I was inspired by holiness and complete dedication to the service of those around them.

The spirituality and charisma of other African American deacons.

Documents of Vatican II.

Sensing a need to expand the clergy in the African American group.

Parable of the talents.

A change in and a new relationship with Christ in my life.

I have always worked in the Church and for the Church, so why not do it as a deacon.

The idea of what the diaconate meant as a sign and symbol of the work that I was already doing, especially as a married man.

I felt that the leadership of the Catholic area I lived in (urban) was not addressing the everyday problems which I faced.

They invited me, since it was the first time a program was initiated. I had already been active in the Church as an altar boy, usher, and minister of communion (extraordinary in those days) and had continued as such until asked to join the program.

Early life experience in Church and school.

Wanted to be a priest.

Before I decided to leave the minor seminary, I visited the Blessed Sacrament and something in my mind said, if not a priest, maybe a deacon.

God dropping hints and my prior decision to do his will.

Father's ministry.

[To make up for] a lack of strong belief in scriptures, a lack of belief in Jesus and truths of Roman Catholic faith, and a lack of education within the Afro American parishes about Roman Catholic faith.

European American priests did not encourage us to believe in our ability to have vibrant, faith-filled parishes, even when we could see the Baptist African Americans with much more faith and self-supporting efforts in the same neighborhoods.

As a married man, I could not become a priest.

Charismatic renewal.

The need for male role models of African American descent.

My faith/Catholic education.

An experience as lay director in the Christ Renews His Parish movement (plus an attraction to the priesthood before marriage).

When asked what the Church can do to attract more African American deacons, several equally important responses were given.

Recruit more aggressively and actively encourage men to consider the diaconate. Especially recruit younger men. Make them feel needed and wanted. Provide them with programs that are indigenous to their culture.

Educate parishes about the diaconate and need for African American deacons. Provide communities and schools with educational programs that utilize audio-video tapes and the media, and which portray African American deacons in action.

Provide opportunities to expose African American deacons more often to the community.
Better utilize gifts of deacons so that they can become better role models of the diaconate. Put deacons in positions of responsibility.

Reduce racism and a eurocentric approach to African American deacons, and be more accepting of African American culture. Provide more Black educational experiences about the culture for the community.

When asked about their greatest joy in studying for/being a deacon, several equally important responses were given:

Getting to know God better/deepening personal spiritual life.

Serving others/ministering to the sick and needy/preaching/ministering sacraments/bringing ministry to the workplace.

Greater personal learning of the scriptures/church history/the Church.

Baptizing grandchildren/working along with wife.

When asked about their greatest sorrow in studying for/being a deacon, a substantial number of deacons reported no sorrow. The most repeated sorrow was nonacceptance by priests. Others pointed to the following:

Church politics/racism.

Reluctance and slow acceptance of minorities.

The non-Christian mentality/behavior of many ordained ministers.

Not doing more.

Not being trained more sufficiently.

Not enough Blacks being attracted to the diaconate.

When asked what, if any, changes deacons would recommend for diocesan diaconate formation programs, the following were reported:

Sensitivity study, so that all people will get to know one another.

Integration of liturgical concepts for meaningful worship in all communities.

Include culture and race sensitivity in training.

Include women in the deacon order.

Train priests to view deacons as ministers called by God to help the Church.

Better focus on ethnicity.

Internships at multicultural parishes.

African American instructors.

Re-evaluate the meaning of service.

More interest in the liturgy and less interest in special ministries of service.

Extend program to four years.

Balance with more internships in various ministries.

Add some classroom time for theology, philosophy, church history, etc.

Have a uniform formation, so that all deacons would have the same basics to perform. We have a deacon's handbook that does that, and it is now accepted by many dioceses.

Have pastors, nuns, and other religious sit in on class.

Black deacons should be used sometimes as instructors.

Put more emphasis on spirituality and not educational background.

Give more sociological and psychological testing of candidates who enter the program to screen them.

Put a little less emphasis on preaching and more on charity and serving the poor.

Use the teaching methods of the seminary, not the weekend retreat method.

Standardize teaching the "how to" things in our ceremonies.

Make pastors aware of the deacon's role in the faith community.

That they be headed by deacons.

That they be in depth in study, prayer, and service.

That formation be relevant to the candidates.

That the formation program be evaluated regularly by the ordained community.

More emphasis on spiritual development.

More well-rounded curriculum.

More practical experience during formation in different ministries.

Scrutinize prospective candidates more closely.

Establish strong relationship with parish priests and religious.

More time for public speaking and homiletics.

That there be two or even three separate but equal programs for different nationalities. There are good deacon-material men out there that won't be tapped, because the educational requirements now are too rigid.

More training in human sexuality.

An admittance on the part of formation staff and majority candidates that racism is still very prevalent and a willingness to face those problems head on.

Shorter, more intensive formation before ordination with continuing education at the local Catholic college after ordination. This should fit the requirements of the ministry the deacon selects.

Currently there is a requirement to have a college degree or equivalent. I think this eliminates many good people, especially immigrants.

Education about the diaconate to parishes, schools, and church agencies. There has been poor public relations to date.

Academic certification and facilitation of earning degrees by candidates/deacons who interface at parishes with very educated staff and volunteers (lay and religious).

Know what the diaconate is and accept deacons as chosen people of God.

Make the use of deacons more effective in sacrament celebrations.

If there is a language problem, use deacons to concelebrate if they speak the language and don't let them stand by the priest as a pole or an imposter.

The use of minimum standards of admission, together with rigid screening.

A strong commitment from spouses.

Emphasis on spiritual guidance.

Eliminate prejudice in instructors for formation.

More philosophy and pastoral ministry.

Some core requirements that would put some commonality in all diaconate formations. There are as many differences in formation programs as there are dioceses.

That the role of the deacon be made known to the priests he is to work with and the people of God he is to serve.

Special training for those deacons scheduled to serve in African American communities.

More "hands on" experiences in the "trenches."

Explaining more of the "why" questions.

A greater concentration on field experiences.

Emphasis placed upon the similarities of the priesthood and diaconate as opposed to the differences.

Attempt to improve the image of the diaconate and the need for deacons.

That all bishops and priests would extend a welcome hand to the aspirant and show them they truly care about their progress in formation instructions.

Faculty to anoint. I am perfectly aware that often anointing is preceded by confession. Still, not everyone who dies is conscious enough to speak.

That the deacons take more of a part in the Mass, for instance at the end of the eucharistic prayer the deacon should at least say "Let us remember those who have died."

Four-year formation.

National standards.

The inclusion of studies on African American culture and its sense of church.

Inclusion of roles played by people of color in the Bible.

To enlarge the formation program so that the needs of all cultures are addressed. At present the formation program director recognizes this need and is moving in a positive manner to address this issue.

There should be, as part of the curriculum in the formation program, a course or program to introduce non-African American brothers to African American culture and heritage, even if they never have to work or serve in an African American setting.

That authentic Christianity be presented and not the make-over that Christianity has become.

Allow African American deacons to be a part of all levels: planning, recruitment, curriculum, and teachers.

Get input from the African American community.

As work in field ministry, place people in Black parishes.

Establish more deacons as directors.

Program directors and instructors should be required to receive formal education in African and African American studies.

Changes are made to a seminary setting so that all deacons will receive similar instruction.

Include study of major ethnic groups in the diocese.

RESEARCH PRIORITIES FOR AFRICAN AMERICAN CULTURE

REV. EUGENE HEMRICK
REV. ROLLINS E. LAMBERT

The aim of this chapter is to suggest research topics on African American culture. Many of these suggestions are based on public policy statements that were approved by the National Black Congress VII and the National Black Clergy Caucus (NBCC) at their 1992 meeting in New Orleans. We have selectively chosen certain issues we feel can be researched realistically and realize many equally important issues exist that we have not addressed. We recommend that the reader revisit the proceedings of the Congress VII and also reread the pastoral *Brothers and Sisters to Us* to experience the full range of issues in need of research.

The more the Church researches African American culture, the better it will serve it, be enriched by its gifts, and attract African Americans of other faiths.

Often research is bypassed by those who do not understand its potential or who fear what it will uncover. Research's primary strength is not in creating controversy, but rather in creating new sensitivi-

ties and insights, while at the same time countering ignorance generated by hearsay. It is positive by nature and aims at cutting through to essentials, educating about future possibilities, and most importantly, creating the dialogue Pope Paul VI's encyclical *Ecclesiam Suam* saw was needed for renewal.

Moreover, research properly conducted on the African American culture has the added power to refute racism and assist the Church in living its commitment to social justice.

First we suggest that more than one type of research be employed when researching the African American culture. The chapters in this book are a good example of the multi-research approach to African American culture. In the demographic work of Dr. Che Fu Lee and Rev. Raymond Potvin, in the sociological studies conducted by Rev. Eugene Hemrick, Dr. Bernard Glos, and Dr. Andrew Billingsley, and in the anthropological research that made possible the chapters on effective African American parishes, we have examples of social science research. In Fr. Cyrian Davis's chapter we are treated to an example of historical research. In Donna Ashaka's and David Gibson's chapters we experience the power of library research.

If the Church hopes to assist the African American culture and its quest for renewal through research, it needs to employ social scientists, historians, librarians, and also theologians and computer scientists.

THE NEED TO NETWORK IN AN ELECTRONIC AGE

The first step to any good research is to gather researchers of repute and learn what they have already accomplished lest the wheel be reinvented.

We therefore suggest that before any research be conducted, a national network of social scientists, historians, theologians, and librarians conversant with the African American culture be established to

- Summarize in one place the results of their work
- Create an interdisciplinary dialogue among African American leaders and church leaders

Furthermore, we see the electronic highway and E-mail systems like Internet being employed as a means for networking this national organization of researchers, for gathering information, and for conducting conferences via the computer.

In studying the electronic highway, we have learned that it has several advantages heretofore not in existence:

- It helps meetings become much more focused and get to the point quicker.
- It offers instantaneous communication, is easy to employ, and is inexpensive.
- It gives one immediate access to large data banks, libraries, and other informational sources.
- It allows people from around the world to communicate easily with each other.
- It has the power of bringing third world nations together with first world nations and makes the universality of the Church more real.

This last advantage is especially in line with the National Black Clergy Conference recommendation: "There is a need to further sensitize ourselves and the entire Church regarding our rich connections with our Black African brothers and sisters, as well as the people who share our African ancestry, the diaspora, throughout the world."

SOCIAL SCIENCE RESEARCH

We suggest that studies be conducted as suggested by the Congress VII which address

- A review of national studies that pertain to successful programs among African American youth.
- The extent to which dioceses and parishes attempt to assist African American males, females, and youth in receiving on-the-job training.
- The extent and successful use of Africentric curricula in Catholic schools.
- The extent and use of Africentric teaching methodologies.
- Successful African American programs that cope with the pressures and issues of our modern society—substance abuse, unemployment, affluence, media, poverty, etc.
- Successful family ministry programs that have grown out of the traditional cultural values of African American life.
- The use of African American lay leadership in parishes.
- The extent and use of African American catechetical materials for home use.

- Successful male role models in African American family life.
- A national profile of African American diocesan offices.
- A national study of African American priests, sisters, brothers, and permanent deacons aimed at learning what prompted their vocation and what they would recommend for increasing African American vocations.

HISTORICAL RESEARCH

Catholic African American history is wide open and yet unexplored. We have learned that the number of Catholic African American historians can be counted on one hand, and that if a person has an attraction to Catholic African American history, there awaits for him or her vast areas of history waiting to be tapped.

We learned, for example, about the Josephite archives in Baltimore under the direction of Fr. Peter Hogan, which contain large amounts of information on Catholic African Americans that are waiting to be turned into innumerable Ph.D. dissertations and books.

In the area of Catholic African American history, we suggest that research be conducted on the role of the Catholic Church during Reconstructionalism. Where did the Church fail as well as successfully respond to those who were slaves? What was behind the failure and success? How did the Catholic faith spread among slaves? What kind of devotional exercises did the slaves use? What tools can one use to uncover the religious consciousness of slaves? What lessons will these findings teach today's Church?

We suggest studies be conducted on the history of evangelization of Black slaves. Where were there examples of effective evangelization? What models were used to evangelize? What were the personalities of those who evangelized like? What part did geography, politics, and the social climate play?

Another topic for historical research is that of African American brotherhoods (the confradias). These brotherhoods were found in Latin America and Brazil and exist to some extent today. Historically, they included Africans and mulattos, male and female, slave and free. It seems they did not exist in what is now U.S. territories. Why is this so?

Several attempts were made to establish congregations of African American religious brothers. Why did they fail?

Some free Blacks as well as slaves formed self-help communities. What is the story behind these communities? Are there any such self-help communities in the present history of the Church?

A number of Black Catholic schools, including boarding schools, were established at the beginning of the century by people like Blessed Katherine Drexel and Fr. John La Farge. What is the history of these institutes? How many of these schools existed?

THEOLOGICAL RESEARCH

As was suggested by Congress VII, studies are needed to determine the desirability and feasibility of establishing an African American Catholic Rite.

Within every culture popular religiosity helps to keep it religiously alive. It is proposed that a study of African American popular religiosity be conducted. What are its roots? What does its world of symbols look like, and what sense of Church does it foster?

THE MORE THE CHURCH RESEARCHES AFRICAN AMERICAN CULTURE, THE BETTER IT WILL SERVE IT, BE ENRICHED BY ITS GIFTS, AND ATTRACT AFRICAN AMERICANS OF OTHER FAITHS.

We further recommend that successful African American liturgies and preaching be studied to learn the causes of their effectiveness.

LIBRARY RESEARCH

It is recommended that a national list of Catholic African American leaders be compiled and that profiles be prepared on them and their accomplishments. Congress VII was very concerned that African Americans increase their pride in their culture by better understanding it. This leads us to the recommendation that existing information and future information on the African American culture be gathered and put on CD-Rom and video so that it can be easily distributed to dioceses and those who serve African American communities. Examples of the power of CD-Rom already exist and suggest great opportunities for the African American culture. For example, one can now purchase CD-Rom talking and video encyclopedias of persons like Martin Luther King delivering his "I Have a Dream" address via computer.

If, as is happening now with much of American history, the history of Catholic African Americans is put on CD-Rom, a young student could sit down at a computer and not only read a text, but also watch and hear historical persons and see historical places.

CONCLUSION

Only an African American can fully appreciate the African American culture to its fullest. We there-fore strongly recommend that most new research on African Americans be conducted by African American researchers.

In line with this recommendation, we suggest that thought be given to creating a corps of Church African Americans as we enter the third millennium and respond to the "new evangelization" to which Pope John Paul II alerts us.

Of all the research that has been recommended above, we strongly recommend that in the future a large percentage be of the participant observation or anthropological variety. In addition to valuable information gathered through questionnaires and in libraries, researchers need to go into the actual situation of a parish or neighborhood and observe first-hand what is happening.

It is through first-hand observation that we can uncover some insights that may fall through the cracks in surveys. The African American culture is filled with meaningful symbolism, much of which needs to be observed to be identified and understood.

If money is to be spent on research, it should not go into broad polling. We believe that fewer but well-done participant studies will be more productive.

ORGANIZATIONS THAT SUPPORT AFRICAN AMERICANS

DONNA ASHAKA

CATHOLIC ORGANIZATIONS AND RESOURCES

EDUCATION

Black Catholic Theological Symposium
c/o Sr. Jamie Phelps, OP, Ph.D.
The Catholic Theological Union
1380 E. Hyde Park Boulevard, Suite 818
Chicago, IL 60615
(312) 324-8000
A community of Black Catholic scholars with doctoral degrees that focuses on scholarly development, acts as a forum for theological scholars, and explores the significance of scholarly work for mission and ministry in the Church in the African American community.

Institute for Black Catholic Studies at Xavier University
Xavier University
934 South Cortez Street
New Orleans, LA 70125-1106
(504) 486-7411
The institute offers an education from the perspective of the Christian faith as expressed in the Black religious community. Offers the only graduate program in the country in Black Catholic theology.

Xavier University
New Orleans, LA 70125
(504) 486-7411
Xavier is the only predominantly Black Catholic university in the world. Founded by Mother Katherine Drexel and the Sisters of the Blessed Sacrament in 1925, Xavier has nineteen departments in its College of Arts and Sciences and offers courses in forty-three major areas of studies.

HEALTH CARE

Association of Black Catholics Against Abortion
1011 First Avenue
New York, NY 10022
(212) 371-1000
A group of African American Catholics opposed to abortion that conduct programs, workshops, and conferences.

MEDIA

The Black Catholic Televangelization Network
5247 Sheridan Avenue
Detroit, MI 48213
(313) 924-4333
A television network that airs and produces, as part of its programming, shows for and about Black Catholics.

In a Word
The Society of the Divine Word
Media Production Center
199 Seminary Drive
Bay St. Louis, MS 39520
(601) 466-4393
A monthly publication featuring articles for and about African Americans, particularly African American Catholics.

Maryknoll Press
Maryknoll Fathers and Brothers
Maryknoll, New York 10545
(914) 941-7590
An organization that publishes the magazine of the Catholic Foreign Mission Society with a significant focus on Africa.

The National Haitian Apostolate Newsletter
221-05 Linden Boulevard
P.O. Box 718
Cambria Heights, NY 11411
(718) 276-4698
A quarterly publication providing news and information on Haiti and Haitian refugees. The publication is printed in both English and French. The Haitian Apostolate runs a national office to coordinate the evangelization of Haitian people nationwide.

Pass It On
Ethnic Communications Outlet
4107 W. 26th Street
Chicago, IL 60623
(312) 522-5151
A one-page insert, designed for personal use or as a bulletin insert, that contains information and resources for and by the African community.

Plenty Good Room
Liturgy Training Publications
Subscription Services
1800 N. Hermitage Avenue
Chicago, IL 60622-1101
(800) 933-4213
A bimonthly magazine on the experiences of African American Catholic worship in the liturgy. Highlights include a showcase of persons in leadership and liturgy planning.

MUSIC

Lead Me Guide Me
GIA Publications, Inc.
7404 S. Mason Avenue
Chicago, IL 60638
(708) 496-3800
An African American Catholic hymnal born of the needs and aspirations of Black Catholics for music that reflects both their Black heritage and the Catholic faith.

RELIGIOUS

Black and Indian Mission Office
2021 H Street, N.W.
Washington, DC 20006
(202) 331-8542
The office is responsible for the National Black and Native American Collection, which focuses on the development, growth, and evangelization of the Black and Native American communities of the Church.

The Drexel Society
506 Woodsmoke Drive
Houston, TX 77013
(713) 450-2306
A service organization dedicated to community service that includes a fund to assist elderly sisters in retirement and Dreams Alive, a program that makes dreams come true for women who live with debilitating health challenges.

National Association of Black Catholic Administrators
Office of Black Catholics
Archdiocese of Washington
P.O. Box 29260
Washington, DC 20017
NABCA is dedicated to providing a forum for Black Catholic administrators to gather and share collective resources and address spiritual needs, issues, and concerns facing the African American communities served.

Knights of Peter Claver and Ladies Auxiliary
National Headquarters
1825 Orleans Avenue
New Orleans, LA 70116
(504) 821-4225
An organization whose goal it is to render service to God and Church by assisting hierarchy and clergy of the Roman Catholic Church by planning and executing works of Catholic Action; being an example to youth; helping the sick; and promoting social and intellectual association among its members.

National African American Catholic Youth Ministry Network
P.O. Box 608
Louisville, KY 40203
(502) 491-0375
NAACYMN implements the youth component of the 1987 National Black Catholic Pastoral Plan and brings together youth ministers from African American Catholic Communities to enhance the growth and development of African American youth and youth ministers.

National Association of African American Catholic Deacons
Our Lady Gate of Heaven Church
8746 S. Harper
Chicago, IL 60619
(312) 375-3059
NAAACD provides a national forum for African American Catholic deacons to promote diaconal unity; address common issues and concerns about their ministry; and further the spiritual and professional growth of African American deacons and their families.

National Black Catholic Clergy Caucus
1733 Andrew J. Brown Avenue
Indianapolis, IN 46202
(317) 632-9349
Serves as a fraternity for Black Catholic clergy and religious to support the spiritual, theological, educational, and ministerial growth of its members; also serves as a vehicle to bring contributions of the Black community to fruition within the Catholic Church.

National Black Catholic Congress, Inc.
320 Cathedral Street
Baltimore, MD 21201
(410) 547-5330
The congress serves to motivate and inspire Catholic leaders to share the Gospel with African Americans, develop methods of evangelization within the context of their social and economic conditions, devise strategies for implementation, and develop an African American Catholic agenda.

National Black Catholic Seminarians Association
Notre Dame Seminary
2901 S. Carrollton Avenue
New Orleans, LA 70118
(504) 861-9142
The NBCSA serves as a means of support for members, who will become ordained priests or religious brothers, and to help meet the cultural needs unique to Black seminarians.

National Black Catholic Sisters' Conference

3027 Fourth Street, N.E.
Washington, DC 20017
(202) 529-9250

The sisters' conference seeks to develop the personal resources of Black women and challenge society, especially the Catholic Church, to address issues of racism in the United States. It maintains educational programs for facilitating change and community involvement in inner-city parochial schools and parishes.

Secretariat for African American Catholics

3211 Fourth Street, N.E.
Washington, DC 20017
(202) 541-3177

The secretariat serves as the chief advisor to the National Conference of Catholic Bishops and the United States Catholic Conference in fulfilling its ministry to African American Catholics in the United States.

RESEARCH

The History of Black Catholics in the United States

Crossroad Publishing
370 Lexington Avenue
New York, NY 10017
(212) 532-3650

A full-length treatment of the Black Catholic experience and African American religious life, written by Fr. Cyprian Davis, OSB, that brings the reader a truer and more inclusive view of the Catholic Church in this country.

The Josephite Pastoral Center

1200 Varnum Street, N.E.
Washington, DC 20017
(202) 526-9270

An educational, research, and pastoral service that develops and shares materials and programs and provides reliable and relatable information regarding African American and Catholic culture.

SECULAR ORGANIZATIONS

BUSINESS

African American Book Distributors

53 W. Jackson Boulevard, Suite 1040
Chicago, IL 60604
(312) 663-0167

A major distributor of African American and third world books.

African American Institute

833 United Nations Plaza
New York, NY 10017
(212) 949-5666

An organization that fosters development in Africa and promotes understanding between Africans and African Americans through development programs, programs that promote policy dialogue and spotlight Africa, and programs that broaden and sustain a constituency for Africa in the United States.

African American Museum Association

P.O. Box 548
Wilberforce, OH 45384-0548
(513) 376-4611

An association that fosters and promotes the celebration and investigation of African and African American cultural heritage by serving the interests of Black museums and related institutions and professionals.

African American Women's Association, Inc.

P.O. Box 55122 - Brightwood Station
Washington, DC 20011
(202) 966-6645

A private, non-profit organization dedicated to the establishment of closer relationships and understanding between the women of Africa and the Americas through cultural, educational, charitable, and social activities.

Africare
440 R Street, N.W.
Washington, DC 20001
(202) 462-3614
A development assistance organization dedicated to improving the quality of life for people who live in rural Africa through programs in agriculture, water resources development, natural resources management, and health.

Afro American Historical and Genealogical Society
P.O. Box 73086 - T Street Station
Washington, DC 20056-3086
(202) 234-5350
A group that encourages scholarly research in Afro-American history and genealogy. Members include anthropologists, historians, sociologists, genealogists, and educators.

American Association of Black Women Entrepreneurs, Inc.
P.O. Box 13933
Silver Spring, MD 20911
(301) 565-0258
An association providing support to Black women business owners through information, professional development training, and networking; promotes the interests of its members through federal, state, and local business development programs.

Blacks in Government
1820 11th Street, N.W.
Washington, DC 20001
(202) 667-3280
A group that promotes the interests of Black civil servants working in federal, state, and local governments. Monitors reductions in force and hiring practices in government agencies.

Black United Front
700 East Oakwood Boulevard
Chicago, IL 60053
(312) 268-7500
An alternative Black organization that works with contacts in Africa and the Caribbean and develops programs to strengthen Black families.

Black Women's Employment Project
99 Hudson Street, 16th Floor
New York, NY 10013
(212) 219-1900
A research and education project that seeks more effective ways to fight discrimination against Black women in employment. It is administered by the NAACP Legal Defense and Educational Fund.

Black Women's Forum
3870 Crenshaw Boulevard
Suite 210
Los Angeles, CA 90008
(213) 292-3009
A platform for discussion of issues of concern to Black women including health, education, welfare, criminal justice, cultural arts, and international affairs.

Booker T. Washington Foundation
4324 Georgia Avenue
Washington, DC 20011
(202) 882-7100
The foundation operates in areas that include resource development, international development and cooperation, science and technology, telecommunications, and public policy research.

Congressional Black Associates, Inc.
U.S. House of Representatives
Room 1979, Longworth House Office Building
Washington, DC 20515
(202) 225-5865
A group made up of present and past employees of the U.S. House of Representatives, the Senate and other related agencies that provides information and analyses on the workings of the federal government to its members and the community through programs, projects, and political education seminars.

Constituency for Africa

c/o Africare
440 R Street, N.W.
Washington, DC 20001
(202) 462-3614
A broad-based coalition of organizations, institutions, and individuals committed to the progress of developing African nations.

Homeland/IBN

1182 Broadway
New York, NY 10001
(212) 447-6678
The largest wholesale provider of African textiles and clothing in the United States.

Institute for the Advanced Study of Black Family Life and Culture, Inc.

P.O. Box 24739
Oakland, CA 94623
(510) 836-3245
A non-profit Black "think tank" and scientific, education, training, and research corporation specializing in the scientific, educational, and cultural aspects of family life and human development.

International Black Women's Congress

1081 Bergen Street, Suite 200
Newark, NJ 07112
(201) 926-0570
IBWC brings together, at an international level, women of African descent for mutual support and socioeconomic empowerment. Their long-term goals include the establishment of an International Black Women's Bank and Fund.

International Black Writers

P.O. Box 1030
Chicago, IL 60690
(312) 924-3818
Founded to meet the needs of Black writers in their efforts to enter and remain in the writing profession.

Johnson Products Company, Inc.

8522 S. Lafayette Avenue
Chicago, IL 60620
(312) 483-4100
A Black hair care products company that also distributes cosmetics targeted to Black women.

Minority Business Enterprise Legal Defense and Education Fund

220 I Street, N.E., Suite 240
Washington, DC 20002
(202) 543-0040
An organization that provides legal assistance and information to support the development of minority-owned businesses.

Minority Network of the American Society for Training and Development, Inc.

1630 Duke Street, Box 1443
Alexandria, VA 22313
(703) 683-8100

National Association of Black Women Attorneys

3711 Macomb Street, N.W.
Washington, DC 20016
(202) 966-9691
A membership organization comprising practicing and retired members of the bar, law students, and paralegals who work toward increased opportunities for minorities within the legal profession.

National Association of Black Women Entrepreneurs

P.O. Box 1375
Detroit, MI 48231
(313) 431-7400
A membership organization of Black women business owners and those interested in starting businesses. Offers workshops and forums and publishes a newsletter.

National Association of Minority Contractors
1333 F Street, N.W., Suite 500
Washington, DC 20004
(202) 347-8259
An educational association that serves as advocate for minority construction contractors. Provides training and procurement opportunities as well as serving as advocate for minority contractors in political forums.

National Association of Negro Business and Professional Women's Clubs, Inc.
1806 New Hampshire Avenue, N.W.
Washington, DC 20009
(202) 483-4206
A support network for Black businesswomen and professionals who are committed to community service. Programs include a focus on education, the elderly, employment, health, housing, monitoring of federal legislation, and programs for youth.

National Black Leadership Roundtable
1025 Connecticut Avenue, N.W., Suite 615
Washington, DC 20036
(202) 331-2030
A membership organization for Black presidents of national organizations who review and act on issues of concern to Black Americans.

National Black United Fund, Inc.
50 Park Place, Suite 1538
Newark, NJ 07102
(201) 643-5122
A fundraising organization that solicits contributions from the Black community and distributes grants to deserving Black organizations involved in cultural programs, economic development, education, health and human services, and social justice programs.

National Black Youth Leadership Council, Inc.
250 West 54th Street, Suite 811
New York, NY 10019
(212) 541-7600
An organization whose focus is on the low retention of Black students in predominately White colleges and offers workshops in the areas of leadership careers, skills, and success training for Black students.

National Black Women's Consciousness Raising Association
1906 North Charles Street
Baltimore, MD 21218
(301) 685-8392
Originally a postoperative support group for Black women, the association has broadened its focus to include a variety of areas of interest to women, including business and education.

National Caucus and Center on Black Aged, Inc.
1424 K Street, N.W., Suite 500
Washington, DC 20005
(202) 637-8400
An organization that serves as an advocate on issues that affect Black elderly populations with Congress and Federal agencies. The caucus also provides employment, training, housing opportunities, and an information clearinghouse.

National Coalition of 100 Black Women
300 Park Avenue, 17th Floor
New York, NY 10022
(212) 974-6140
A community service and advocacy organization that seeks to empower Black women through programs, networking, and building links between the organization and the corporate and political arenas, thereby making Black women more visible in the socioeconomic and political sectors.

National Minority Business Council, Inc.

235 East 42nd Street
New York, NY 10017
(212) 537-2385
The Council assists minority-owned companies in the areas of advocacy, communication, education, international trade, procurement, and training.

National Urban Affairs Council

2350 Adam Clayton Powell Boulevard
New York, NY 10030
(914) 694-4000
The council identifies common interests of the public and private sectors and the Black community that promote mutual economic growth; monitors legislation that affects the Black community; and serves as a liaison for Black organizations.

National Urban Coalition

8601 Georgia Avenue
Silver Spring, MD 20910
(202) 495-4999
The coalition's focus is on issues such as drugs, employment, health, and housing; particularly seeks solutions to problems of urban school systems and minorities.

One Hundred Black Men

105 East 22nd Street
New York, NY 10010
(212) 777-7070
An organization that provides mentoring and support to young Black men and provides scholarships for college.

Operations Crossroads Africa

150 Fifth Avenue, Suite 310
New York, NY 10011
(212) 242-855
A program to help bridge the gap between the United States and Africa through programs offering work, study, and travel experiences.

United Black Fund of America, Inc.

1012 14th Street, N.W., Suite 300
Washington, DC 20005
(800) 323-7677
A fundraising organization that coordinates efforts to assist social service programs serving the Black population.

World Africa Chamber of Commerce

1725 K Street, N.W., Suite 410
Washington, DC 20006
(202) 223-3244
An organization that promotes development through increased trade between the United States and Africa.

CIVIL RIGHTS

A. Phillip Randolph Institute

260 Park Avenue, South
New York, NY 10010
(212) 533-8000
An organization that promotes increased political involvement of Blacks at the local, state, and national levels of government; increases Black activity in the labor movement; and fosters the development of trade unionism in the Black community.

Congress of Racial Equality

30 Cooper Square, 9th Floor
New York, NY 10003
(212) 598-4000
A major player in the civil rights movement during the 1960s, today CORE is working on more subtle and unsuspecting forms of racism and discrimination and concentrating on economic development, education, job training, and after-school programs.

Lawyers' Committee for Civil Rights Under the Law

1400 Eye Street, N.W., Suite 400
Washington, DC 20005
(202) 371-1212
The committee provides legal representation to the minority and poor in cases of discrimination as it relates to education, employment, and municipal service.

Martin Luther King Center for Nonviolent Social Change, Inc.

449 Auburn Avenue, N.E.
Atlanta, GA 30312
(404) 524-1956

The center was established to preserve and advance Dr. King's unfinished work through teaching, interpreting, advocating, and promoting nonviolence in the elimination of poverty, racism, and violence.

National Association for the Advancement of Colored People (NAACP)

4805 Mount Hope Drive
Baltimore, MD 21215
(410) 358-8900

The largest civil rights organization in the world, the NAACP is the national spokesman for Black Americans and other minorities and for those who support civil rights objectives in America. The NAACP articulates the grievances of Black Americans and protects their rights by whatever legal means necessary.

NAACP Legal Defense and Educational Fund, Inc.

National Office
99 Hudson Street, Suite 1600
New York, NY 10013-2897

A fully tax-exempt national civil rights law firm known as the legal arm of the civil rights movement. The fund has participated in numerous civil rights cases, winning hundreds of victories in the United States Supreme Court.

National Council of Negro Women, Inc.

1667 K Street, N.W., Suite 700
Washington, DC 20006
(202) 659-0006

NCNW is the largest organization dedicated to African American women and their families. For more than 57 years they have been in the forefront of the fight for civil rights, teaching values of unity, self-reliance, individual worth and dignity, education, and strong family ties.

National Urban League

500 East 62nd Street
New York, NY 10021
(212) 310-9000

The league is one of the major organizations seeking civil rights for minorities and conducting programs in areas that include education, health, and job training.

ECONOMY

American League of Financial Institutions

1709 New York Avenue, N.W., Suite 801
Washington, DC 20006
(202) 628-5624

A membership organization comprised of 51 Black-, Hispanic-, Asian American-, and female-owned/managed savings and loans institutions that promotes thrift and home ownership among minority groups and conducts programs to stimulate the growth of minority-owned savings and loans.

Caribbean-American Chamber of Commerce and Industry, Inc.

Brooklyn Navy Yard Building, Suite 5
Mezzanine "A"
Brooklyn, NY 11215
(718) 834-4544

An organization formed to promote economic development among Caribbean-American businesses, as well as other minority-owned businesses.

National Association of Black and Minority Chambers of Commerce

5741 Telegraph
Oakland, CA 94609
(415) 601-5741

A group of agencies that coordinates business development activities for Blacks and minorities.

Minority Business Enterprise

Legal Defense and Education Fund
220 Eye Street, Suite 280
Washington, DC 20002
(202) 543-0040
An organization providing legal assistance and information to support minority-owned businesses.

Minority Business Information Institute, Inc.

130 Fifth Avenue
New York, NY 10011
(212) 242-8000
A networking organization that keeps minorities abreast of information, resources, and groups that could be helpful in business and professional endeavors.

EDUCATION

Associations of Black Admissions and Financial Aid Officers of Ivy League and Sister Schools

P.O. Box 1402
Cambridge, MA 02238-1402
(401) 863-2378
An association that works to improve the methods of recruitment, selection, and financial aid for minority students at the ivy league and sister schools.

Association of Black Women in Higher Education, Inc.

Fashion Institute
Office of Academic Affairs
227 W. 27th Street, Suite c-913
New York, NY 10001
An association established to foster and expand the role of Black women in higher education and to provide a vehicle for supporting their aims and goals in professional development.

Black Caucus of the American Library Association

c/o Virginia State Library
11th Street at Capitol Square
Richmond, VA 23219
An organization established to call attention to the needs of the Black community regarding information access and to facilitate library services that meet the information needs of Black people.

Institute for the Advanced Study of Black Family Life and Culture

155 Filbert Street, Suite 202
Oakland, CA 94607
(415) 836-3245
A research organization focusing on the needs of Black families.

Institute for Independent Education

1313 N. Capitol Street, NE
Washington, DC 20002
(202) 745-0500
A technical assistance and policy development organization serving more than 300 independent neighborhood schools in America's inner cities and approximately 52,000 African American students in 30 states, the District of Columbia, and the Virgin Islands.

National Alliance Against Racist and Political Repression

126 W. 119th Street - Suite 101
New York, NY 10026
(212) 866-8600
An educational organization that seeks to end racism and political repression.

National Alliance of Black School Educators

2816 Georgia Avenue, Suite 4
Washington, DC 20001
(202) 483-8323
It is the mission of NABSE to enhance and facilitate the education of Black people by developing leadership and influencing education policies.

National Association for Equal Opportunity in Higher Education

Lovejoy Building
400 12th Street, N.E., Room 207
Washington, DC 20002
(202) 543-9111

A voluntary independent association founded by historically Black colleges and universities organized to articulate the need for a higher education system where race, income, and previous education are not determinants of the quantity or quality of higher education.

National Council for Black Studies

Ohio State University
1800 Cannon Drive
1030 Lincoln Towers
Columbus, OH 43210
(614) 291-1035

A membership organization working to establish standards and provide development guidance for Black Studies programs. It facilitates recruitment of Black scholars for teaching and research; assists in creation of multicultural education; conducts Afrocentric research; and provides resources and advice to policy makers.

Office for the Advancement of Public Black Colleges

1 Dupont Circle, Suite 710
Washington, DC 20036
(202) 778-0818

A membership organization that works for the visibility and private financial support of the thirty-four public Black American colleges.

Voter Education Project, Inc.

604 Beckwith Street, S.W.
Atlanta, GA 30314
(404) 522-7495

A nonpartisan organization that seeks full voting rights for minorities and encourages the use of those rights. Operates a clearinghouse with information on population trends, voting statistics, and minorities in public offices.

The Carter G. Woodson Foundation

P.O. Box 1025, G9, Lincoln Park
Newark, NJ 07101
(202) 242-0500

A multidisciplinary performing arts organization whose mission is to research, preserve, perpetuate, and celebrate the creative expressions, cultural heritage, and historic achievements of African American artists through performances, exhibits, and educational activities throughout the United States.

United Negro College Fund

500 East 62nd Street
New York, NY 10021
(212) 326-1100

A fundraising organization that supports the forty-one historically Black colleges and universities in the United States.

FRATERNITIES

Alpha Phi Alpha Fraternity, Inc.

2313 St. Paul Street
Baltimore, MD 21218
(410) 554-0040

A fraternity that supports community service endeavors that includes promotion of academic excellence as well as a commitment to the disadvantaged.

Kappa Alpha Psi

2322-24 N. Broad Street
Philadelphia, PA 19132
(215) 228-7184

A fraternity that sponsors charitable, educational, and youth programs, and provides scholarships and awards.

Omega Psi Phi

3951 Snapsinger Parkway
Decatur, GA 30035
(404) 284-5533

A fraternity that sponsors community service projects, fosters leadership skills, and provides awards and scholarships to its members.

Phi Beta Sigma

145 Kennedy Street, N.W.
Washington, DC 20011
(202) 726-5424
A service fraternity that has established programs in the areas of education, housing, finance, and youth.

Sigma Pi Phi Fraternity

920 Broadway, Suite 703
New York, NY 10010
(212) 477-5550
A fraternity that supports social and educational programs through sponsorship and scholarships.

HEALTH

Association of Black Cardiologists

3201 Del Paso Boulevard, Suite 100
Sacramento, CA 95815
(916) 641-2224
A group of physicians and health care professionals seeking to improve and promote prevention and treatment of cardiovascular diseases.

Association of Black Psychologists

P.O. Box 55999
Washington, DC 20040
(202) 722-0808
A membership organization that seeks to unite Black professionals and students of psychology to enhance the psychological well-being of Black people in America.

Black Health

P.O. Box 36
Danbury, CT 06813
(203) 909-9387
A quarterly publication focusing on Black health issues.

Black Psychiatrists of America

2730 Adeline Street
Oakland, CA 94607
(415) 465-1800
An organization that serves as a resource for information, education, and training on the mental health needs of the Black population.

National Dental Association

5506 Connecticut Avenue, N.W., Suite 24
Washington, DC 20015
(202) 244-7555
NDA is the largest organization of Black dentists in the world; provides a national forum for Black dentists in the United States.

National Association of Black Social Workers, Inc.

15231 West McNichols Avenue
Detroit, MI 48235
(313) 836-0210
An association designed to promote the welfare, survival, and liberation of the Black community. Members recognize the necessity of Black community control and accountability of self. NABSW offers linkages through its members with all Blacks, having an open membership not predicated upon degrees or experience.

National Association for Sickle Cell Disease, Inc.

3345 Wilshire Boulevard, Suite 1106
Los Angeles, CA 90010-1880
(213) 736-5455
An association organized to create awareness of the impact of sickle cell conditions and to coordinate a national effort to develop and implement programs for persons with these conditions.

National Medical Association

1012 10th Street, N.W.
Washington, DC 20001
(202) 347-1895
A professional association for Black physicians with a focus on improved medical services and increased opportunity in the medical profession.

Research Foundation for Ethnic Related Diseases

2231 South Western Avenue
Los Angeles, CA 90018
(213) 737-7372
A resource organization dealing with sickle cell anemia and other ethnic-related diseases.

MEDIA

The Afro-American Newspaper

628 North Eutaw Street
Baltimore, MD 21201
(301) 383-3219
In existence for more than a hundred years, the *Afro* publishes news and information for and about African Americans. The *Afro* also produces two magazines, *Dawn* and *Every Wednesday*.

Black Awareness in Television

13217 Livernois Street
Detroit, MI 48238-3162
(313) 931-3427
An organization founded to promote African American ideas to the general public and affirmative action in the media and to assist Black groups in their interactions with the electronics media.

The Black Collegian Magazine

1240 South Broad Street
New Orleans, LA 70125
A quarterly publication targeting African American students and focusing on career planning and self-development.

Black Congressional Monitor

P.O. Box 75035
Washington, DC 20013
(202) 244-8879
A monthly report on legislative issues in the U.S. Congress pertaining to African Americans.

Black Enterprise Magazine

Earl G. Graves Publishing Co., Inc.
130 Fifth Avenue
New York, NY 10011-4399
(800) 727-7777
A monthly business-service magazine for African American professionals, corporate executives, middle managers, entrepreneurs, and policy makers in both the public and private sectors.

Black Entertainment Television

1232 31st Street, N.W.
Washington, DC 20007
(202) 337-5260
BET is the nation's first and only basic cable programming service specifically targeting the interests and concerns of Black Americans.

Black Issues in Higher Education

10520 Warwick Avenue
Suite B-8
Fairfax, VA 22030
(703) 385-2981
A comprehensive publication detailing the concerns of women, Hispanics, Asians, Native Americans, and African Americans to higher education decision-makers.

Black Newspapers Clipping Service

42 Macomb Place
New York, NY 10039
(212) 491-9031
A business that scans Black-oriented newspapers and magazines for articles of interest and publishes the *Black Press Periodical Directory*.

The Black Scholar
485 65th Street
Oakland, CA 94609
A quarterly publication focusing on Black studies
and research.

Essence Communications
1500 Broadway
New York, NY 10036
(212) 730-4260
A publishing company that produces *Essence,* a
monthly magazine dedicated to experiences of
African American women, including courage and
conviction, political savvy, business acumen, fashion, and beauty.

Johnson Publishing Company
1820 South Michigan Avenue
Chicago, IL 60605
(312) 322-9200
A landmark African American publishing company
that produces *Ebony, Jet,* and *Ebony Man* magazines.

Journal of Negro Education
Howard University
P.O. Box 311
Washington, DC 20059
(202) 806-8120
In publication for more than fifty years, the journal
deals with new strategies and philosophies for the
education of Black people.

Minority Business Report
Station WGN-TV
2507 W. Bradley Place
Chicago, IL 60618
(312) 222-9012
A weekly television show, shown on cable net-
works, that focuses on minority business news.

Motown Industries
6255 West Sunset Boulevard
Los Angeles, CA
(213) 468-3500
A landmark institution in the record industry that
has produced a roster of popular Black artists and
remains a vital force in the Black music industry
today.

National Association of Black Journalists
P.O. Box 17212
Washington, DC 20041
(703) 648-1270
A membership organization that seeks to increase
professionalism among its members and to open up
opportunities for Black journalists.

National Association of Black Owned Broadcasters, Inc.
1730 M Street, N.W., Suite 412
Washington, DC 20036
An organization that represents the concerns of
Black radio station owners and works to break
down the barriers that prevent Black ownership,
including insufficient capital.

National Black Media Coalition
38 New York Avenue, N.E.
Washington, DC 20002
(202) 387-8155
A membership coalition of primarily Black mass
communications businesses whose focus is visibility
and equity among broadcasters and publishers.

Who's Who Among Black Americans
Gale Research Company
835 Penobscot Building
Detroit, MI 48226
(313) 961-2242
A biannual publication on notable Black
Americans.

The World Institute of Black Communications, Inc.

10 Columbus Circle
New York, NY 10019
(212) 586-1771

An organization that focuses on improving sensitivity to the concerns of Black audiences and increased employment options for minorities in the communication field.

Visions Foundation

1538 Ninth Street, N.W.
Washington, DC 20001
(202) 462-1779

A media and educational foundation established to promote understanding of African American culture. Publications include *American Visions: The Magazine of Afro-American Culture, Afro-American Art,* and *Lines of Sight.*

POLITICAL

Association of Black American Ambassadors

1601 Kalmia Road, N.W.
Washington, DC 20012
(202) 806-5951

An association that works to increase public understanding of diplomacy and provide a forum for exchange of views between its members and various government entities for shaping foreign policy.

Bethune-DuBois Fund

600 New Hampshire Avenue, N.W.
Washington, DC 20037
(202) 625-7048

An organization established to expand the participation and empowerment of African Americans in the political process.

Congressional Black Caucus

House Annex Number 2, Room 344
Third and D Streets, S.W.
Washington, DC 20515
(202) 226-7790

A body composed of forty Black Members of Congress (ten women and thirty men) who, in addition to addressing the concerns of their own particular districts, serve as advocates for the interests of African Americans and other underrepresented populations through their vast legislative agenda.

708-210-9574

Congressional Black Caucus Foundation, Inc.

1004 Pennsylvania Avenue, S.E.
Washington, DC 20003
(202) 675-6730

A foundation that supports and conducts nonpartisan research, technical assistance, training, education, and informational activities and programs to advance political participation by African Americans and other minority group members.

National Association of Minority Political Women

6120 Oregon Avenue, N.W.
Washington, DC 20015
(202) 686-1216

A nonpartisan association whose primary goal is to train minority women and families in understanding politics on the local, regional, and national levels and how to make politics work for their individual and group interests.

National Black Caucus of Local Elected Officials

1301 Pennsylvania Avenue, N.W., Suite 400
Washington, DC 20004
(202) 626-3567

The caucus represents the concerns of Black elected officials of cities and counties in the United States.

National Black Caucus of State Legislators

444 North Capitol Street, N.W., Suite 206
Washington, DC 20001
(202) 624-5457
A membership organization of Black members of state legislatures networking to develop positions on issues of concern to the Black community.

National Black Republican Council

440 First Street, N.W., Suite 409
Washington, DC 20001
(202) 662-1335
The council was established by Republicans in the House and Senate to deal with issues and legislation that impacts the Black community, including business, employment, education, and housing.

National Coalition on Black Voter Participation

1101 14th Street, N.W., Suite 925
Washington, DC 20005
(202) 898-2220
A political organization dedicated to increasing Black voter registration and participation.

TransAfrica

1744 R Street, N.W.
Washington, DC 20009
(202) 779-2301
A lobby group for Africa and the Caribbean in U.S. foreign policy.

RELIGIOUS

Black Biblical Heritage

Winston-Derek Publishers, Inc.
Pennywell Drive, P.O. Box 90883
Nashville, TN 37209
A reference containing historical information on 121 biblical characters who were African or of African descent and other facts from major historians and Biblical scholars concerning historical Africa.

Black Women in Church and Society

c/o Interdenominational Church and Society
671 Beckwith Street, S.W.
Atlanta, GA 30314
(404) 527-7740
An organization that provides leadership training and develops support structures to help women in fulfilling responsibilities brought on by their increased participation in religious and nonreligious activities in the United States and in the Third World; developed a research-resource center on "Black Women and Religion."

Encyclopedia of African-American Religions

c/o Garland Publishing
100A Sherman Avenue
Hamden, CT 06514
A publication with a focus on Black spiritual movements, past and present. A comprehensive reference work on African American religious leaders and groups, and the major aspects, concerns, issues, and expressions of African American religious life.

Gospel Music Workshop of America, Inc.

P.O. Box 4632
Detroit, MI 48234
(313) 989-2340
A membership organization created to promote spiritual and Gospel music.

Research Center on Black Religious Bodies

c/o Howard University School of Divinity
1400 Shepherd Street, N.E.
Washington, DC 20017
(202) 806-0750
A research group that produced the *Directory of African American Religious Bodies*.

RESEARCH

African American Resource Center

P.O. Box 746
Howard University
Washington, DC 20059
(202) 806-7242
The center houses a collection of old and rare publications on various subjects pertaining to Blacks.

African Influence

686 W. Ventura Street
Altadena, CA 91001
(818) 794-7586

A membership organization that encourages individuals to do personal research into African culture and history. Its members also network with others in the United States, Africa, and the Caribbean. The goal is to share information with young people in urban communities.

Association of Black Sociologists

Department of Sociology and Anthropology
Howard University
Washington, DC 20059
(202) 806-6853

The association facilitates research on the Black experience and publicizes findings in professional journals. Recruits new people into the field and provides outlets for their work.

Association for the Study of Afro-American Life and History

1407 14th Street, N.W.
Washington, DC 20005
(202) 667-2822

An organization that collects, researches, preserves, and promotes the achievements and contributions of Black people.

Bethune Museum and Archives, Inc.

1318 Vermont Avenue, N.W.
Washington, DC 20005
(202) 332-1233

The archives houses the papers of the National Council of Negro Women, twentieth century Black women's organizations, and individual Black women. In addition, the archives carries an extensive index of photograph and subject files.

Encyclopedia of African American Religions

c/o Garland Publishing
100A Sherman Avenue
Hamden, CT 06514

A publication with a focus on Black spiritual movements, past and present. A comprehensive reference work on African American religious leaders and groups and the major aspects, concerns, issues, and expressions of African American religious life.

Fisk University Library and Media Center

Special Collections
17th Avenue North
Nashville, TN 37203
(615) 329-8730

The center is one of the most extensive repositories in the field, with more than 36,000 volumes in its Special Negro Collection, covering all aspects of the Black, African, and Caribbean experience dating from the eighteenth century to the present.

Joint Center for Political and Economic Studies

1301 Pennsylvania Avenue, N.W., Suite 400
Washington, DC 20003
(202) 626-3500

The joint center uses research and information dissemination to accomplish three objectives: to improve the socioeconomic status of Black Americans; to increase their influence in the political and public policy arenas; and to facilitate the building of coalitions across racial lines.

Moorland-Spingarn Research Center

Howard University
Washington, DC 20059
(202) 806-7241

The center is a major research facility that houses private collections including an anti-slavery collection and a large collection of books, pamphlets, and manuscripts.

Murray Resource Directory to the Nation's
Historically Black Colleges and Universities
c/o Logical Expression in Design, Inc.
1730 M Street, N.W., Suite 407
Washington, DC 20036
(202) 429-6920
A 322-page guide to 104 Black institutions with
background statements, histories, and missions as
well as a description of the curriculums, campus
environments, financial aid, and admission requirements.

Schomburg Center for Research in Black Culture

515 Lenox Avenue
New York, NY 10037
(212) 862-4000
The center is one of the most widely used research
facilities in the world devoted to the preservation of
materials on Black life.

SOCIAL SERVICES

Associated Black Charities

105 East 22nd Street, Suite 915
New York, New York 10010
(212) 777-6060
ABC is a nonprofit federation of health and human
service agencies. Member agencies serve the needi-
est communities by contributing to their long-term
improvement and enrichment; encourage volun-
teerism and giving; and cooperate with existing
efforts to enhance the overall well-being of Black
communities.

Black Student Leadership Network

25 E Street, N.W.
Washington, DC 20001
(202) 628-87878
The network is a national body of young, Black college student and community-based activists united
in an effort to improve the life chances of this
nation's Black children through effective
community service and advocacy.

Children's Defense Fund

122 C Street, N.W.
Washington, DC 20001
(202) 628-8787
An organization that provides a strong, effective
voice for all American children, particularly the
poor, minority, and disabled. The goal is to educate
the nation about the needs of children and encourage preventive investment before they get sick,
drop out of school, suffer family breakdown, or get
into trouble.

Black Community Crusade for Children

25 E Street, N.W.
Washington, DC 20001
(202) 628-8787
An intensive effort to mobilize the African
American community on behalf of Black children
and families by communicating the crises and steps
that must be taken for positive outcomes; by building effective, informed leadership; and by encouraging, supporting, and promoting effective programs,
policies, and initiatives.

Concerned Black Men

National Chapter
7200 N. 21st Street
Philadelphia, PA 19138
A nonprofit organization of male volunteers who
provide positive male role models and build
stronger channels of communication between
adults and children.

National Black Child Development Institute

1023 15th Street, N.W., Suite 600
Washington, DC 20005
(202) 387-1281
A national nonprofit organization dedicated to
improving the quality of life for African American
children and youth; provides and supports programs, workshops, and resources for African
American children, their parents, and communities
in the areas of child care, health care, education,
and child welfare.

Progressive Life Center, Inc.
1123 11th Street, N.W.
Washington, DC 20001
A nonprofit human services forum that provides a wide range of psychological services to individuals, couples, families, and organizations. Provides development training and organization enhancement services to public, private, and government organizations using Africentric and humanistic models of intervention.

SORORITIES

Alpha Kappa Alpha
5656 S. Stony Island Avenue
Chicago, IL 60637
(312) 684-1282
A service sorority that provides community services, awards, and scholarships and is active with youth.

Alpha Pi Chi
P.O. Box 255
Kensington, MD 20895
(310) 559-4330
A service sorority of business and professional women that conducts fund raising for Black charities and civil rights organizations. It also provides awards and scholarships.

Delta Sigma Theta
1707 New Hampshire Avenue, N.W.
Washington, DC 20009
(202) 986-2400
A public service organization with a five-point program that includes economic development, educational development, international awareness, political awareness and involvement, and physical and mental health awareness.

Sigma Gamma Rho Sorority, Inc.
8800 South Stony Island Avenue
Chicago, IL 60617
(312) 873-9000
An organization whose focus is community service, leadership training, and education of youth. It provides scholarships to students, programs, and projects including Project Africa.

Zeta Phi Beta
1734 New Hampshire Avenue, N.W.
Washington, DC 20009
(202) 387-3103
A service and social organization whose programs focus on youth, senior citizens, the Black male, illiteracy, child care, voter registration, and alcohol and drug abuse.

BIBLIOGRAPHY

For more information about African American Catholics, the following primary sources of information are suggested.

CATECHETICS

Jones, Nathan. *Sharing the Old, Old Story*. Winona: St. Mary's Press, 1982. No longer in print, but back issues may be available.

Lumas, Sr. Eva M., Ph.D., ThM. *Tell It Like It Is: A Black Catholic Perspective on Christian Education*. Washington, D.C.: The National Black Sisters' Conference, 1987. No longer in print, but back issues may be available.

United States Catholic Conference. *Families: Black and Catholic, Catholic and Black*. Washington, D.C.: United States Catholic Conference, 1985.

United States Catholic Conference. *God Bless Them. . . African American Catechetical Camp Meetin': A Gathering to Chart a New Course*. Washington, D.C.: United States Catholic Conference, 1995.

EVANGELIZATION

National Conference of Catholic Bishops. *Here I Am, Send Me*. Washington, D.C.: United States Catholic Conference, 1989.

National Black Catholic Congress, Inc. *A Balm in Gilead: Programs for Parish Implementation*. Baltimore: The National Black Catholic Congress, Inc., 1992.

African American Bishops of the United States. *What We Have Seen and Heard*. Cincinnati: St. Anthony Messenger Press, 1984.

HISTORY

Davis, Rev. Cyprian, OSB. *The History of Black Catholics*. New York: Crossroad Publishing Company, 1990.

United States Catholic Conference. *The Cypress Will Grow*. Washington, D.C.: United States Catholic Conference, 1989 (video and discussion guide).

United States Catholic Conference. *Many Rains Ago*. Washington, D.C.: United States Catholic Conference, 1990.

LITURGY

Secretariat of the Bishops Committee on the Liturgy. *In Spirit and Truth*. Washington, D.C.: United States Catholic Conference, 1989.

Secretariat for the Liturgy and Secretariat for African American Catholics. *Plenty Good Room*. Washington, D.C.: United States Catholic Conference, 1991.

GIA Publications, Inc. *Lead Me, Guide Me. The African American Catholic Hymnal*. Chicago: GIA Publications, 1987.

RACISM

Bishops' Committee on African American Catholics. *Brothers and Sisters to Us*. Washington, D.C.: United States Catholic Conference, 1979.

Bishops' Committee on African American Catholics. *For the Love of One Another*. Washington, D.C.: United States Catholic Conference, 1989.